SQUASH

The Skills of the Game

David Pearson

The Crowood Press

First published in 2001 by
The Crowood Press Ltd
Ramsbury, Marlborough
Wiltshire SN8 2HR

www.crowood.com

This impression 2006

British Library Cataloguing-in-Publication Data
A catalogue record for this book is available from the British Library.

ISBN 1 86126 421 6
EAN 978 1 86126 421 3

Line drawings by Annette Findlay

Typeset by Florence Production Ltd, Stoodleigh, Devon

Printed and bound by The Cromwell Press, Trowbridge, Wiltshire.

Contents

ABOUT THE AUTHOR

David Pearson is England National Coach for the Squash Rackets Association, responsible with others these days for the elite application of a million-pound lottery funded World Class Performance Programme. In a personal history that includes England International status as a player and long one-to-one coaching experience both in the UK and North America, he has had a hand in the development of a generation of top stars, both men and women. Peter Nicol and Cassie Campion benefited from his unusual ability to analyze and improve racket technique and movement on court before going on to dominate the world game. The two top men in England, Simon Parke and Paul Johnson were similarly set on their roads to professional success by his tuition early in their careers.

His involvement in the England men winning the World Team Championship for the first time and then successfully defending the title, and in the England women recovering their World Team Championship after ten years in the shadow of Australia, led to Pearson receiving the prestigious Mussabini Medal from the National Coaching Association, followed by induction into the NCF Hall of Fame.

Colin McQuillan, his collaborator in this book, is squash correspondent to *The Times* and Chief Reporter for *SquashNow!*, the world's leading news-based squash website. He has followed the game at all competitive levels for more than two decades and is an addicted club player. He watched and reported on the world scene when Geoff Hunt, Jonah Barrington and Heather McKay still ruled the game; saw the five-and-a-half-year unbeaten run of Jahangir Khan at close quarters; catalogued the evolution of Jansher Khan as the game's greatest technician; and witnessed the emergence of players like Chris Dittmar, Ross Norman, Susan Devoy, Rodney Eyles, the extraordinary Martin family (Rodney, Brett and Michelle), Nicol, Campion and a host of others.

David Pearson.

Acknowledgements

This book is essentially an attempt to bring squash coaching literature into the modern era. There have been many excellent coaching books in the past, not least under this title, but all of them were based on techniques developed for wooden rackets and courts without air-conditioning of any kind.

Rackets are hardly recognizable today in comparison to the Maxply and Light Blue wooden models of yesteryear. Made from plastic materials developed for space flight and downhill skiing, they are larger, lighter and quicker in the hand, giving greater power on the ball for far less effort and swing, and a manoeuvrability in the front court that previous-era shot players like Qamar Zaman or Dean Williams would have died for.

Courts also have changed almost beyond recognition. Top professional squash is played on all-transparent glass or Perspex courts that display to an audience every facet of their performance from all sides. Clubs have glass-backed courts as standard and coloured courts are increasingly providing a warmer and friendlier atmosphere.

Air-flow heating and air-conditioning are the norm now rather than the often noisy and cumbersome heaters and fans of quite recent history. Just as writers have been forced to replace their old typing techniques with computer skills, so squash players need to reassess their approach to space age equipment. More importantly, perhaps, they need to take on board the new science-based background to all sport preparation.

Although this book carries my byline, it would be dishonest not to acknowledge the input and contribution (often to a point not far short of plagiarism) of others involved in England's National Performance Group who have helped with the chapters on specialist training: Paul Carter my Assistant National Performance Coach with the SRA, for his grasp of competitive tactics and practice; Kirsten Barnes for her detailed description of the role of psychology in modern sport; Damon Brown of The Centre for Sport and Exercise Science at Sheffield's Hallam University for his contribution of physical preparation; Stafford Murray of The University of Wales in Cardiff for his thoughts on the place of video recording in modern squash coaching and his help with photography.

This is the sort of support team any athlete needs behind him to progress to the upper levels of any game today and even club coaches should be seeking to tap into such similar expertise as is available to them within their own areas of operation.

Finally I want to thank Colin McQuillan, the squash correspondent of *The Times*, for his editorial management of this book and his help in making sense of so many thoughts from so many people towards the creation of a manual that makes available for players of all levels the route to the skills of modern squash. NB: While we refer throughout the book to players in the masculine, for continuity, we are thinking of the many women who play squash today; and where we talk of or illustrate forehand and backhand techniques, we are thinking of both right- and left-handed players unless otherwise stated.

David Pearson

CHAPTER 1

The Last Great Fighting Game

INTRODUCTION

There is a common misconception that squash is close kin to other racket sports. In fact, its only relationship to tennis, real tennis, badminton or table tennis lies in the hand-to-eye co-ordination required to apply a striking surface to a flying object – a similarity that might just as easily be drawn with cricket or baseball.

The only game that contains the same demands and elements as squash is its progenitor: rackets, a pursuit that is similarly based upon territorial domination and the manoeuvring of an opponent into positions from which he will find the maximum difficulty in retrieving the next shot. There are winning shots in squash: dead nicks and floor-hugging kill-drives, but most of the contest is about setting the opponent up for the spatial *coup de grâce*.

Unlike the other racket games, squash is about the placing of the returning ball rather than of the actual delivery forward from the racket face. Accepting that the front wall of the squash court is the equivalent of the net in other racket games, only experience and familiarity with the behaviour of the ball within the physical confinement of the court can provide the player with the armoury to play effectively against an opponent who is on the same side of the net. Chess is the analogy many commentators reach for when approaching the basic tactics of the game, but actually the closest relative to squash is

boxing. Physically, the battle for domination of a small, enclosed arena is the same, the balance of the body and the movement to control the centre ground while continuously punishing an opponent forced to travel greater distances than oneself, is similar. The transfer of body weight through the delivery of the shot (punch) and the recovery to balance, often around the body of the advancing opponent, is largely the same.

Mentally the parallels are even closer. Squash is almost impossible to play socially; it is necessary to 'own the court', to punish the opponent when any opening appears, to seek to inflict pain and exhaustion continuously in pursuit of collapse (knock-out), to seek increasingly to damage the opponent as weariness sets in and he becomes more vulnerable. Squash is the last great fighting game: boxing without brain damage!

Increased fitness and athleticism among top professionals has triggered moves towards a lower tin (the tin is a 21in board, usually hollow or made of metal and intended to sound upon impact) and different scoring systems at the upper levels of the game, but squash evolved from its origins in rackets as a nine-point, hand-in hand-out contest which at normal fitness levels provides a wonderful balance of guile and athleticism within a framework that allows for the ebb and flow of both attack and defence. We shall set our thoughts in the unchanged traditional format of the game.

Its origins are somewhat mysterious, but it seems certain that the game of rackets, a faster, harder and more constantly aggressive game, developed in the walled courtyards of the City of London, particularly in prisons such as The Fleet, and was perfected in the public schools such as Harrow and Eton. For a fuller account of these developments there is no better than that by Rex Bellamy in his *Squash: A History*.[1]

What is significant here is the fact that 'squash rackets' emerged as a junior version of 'rackets' when smaller and younger players found that, by puncturing a full rackets ball, they could produce a slower, 'softer' ball more suited to their weaker and less honed abilities. More experienced players came to realize that the 'squashy' ball worked well as a warm-up tool, easing the body into full flow without jarring the muscles or extending the lungs as was necessary with the full competitive 'hard' ball. Nowadays it is the old rackets ball that tends to be confined largely to Britain's public schools and clubs, while the squash balls employed by millions of players around the world are manufactured in varying grades of bounce and speed to service abilities of every level. The World Squash Federation in 1999 officially accepted a new Dunlop range of balls that set the standards for the game.

The principles of the game have never changed, however. Essentially, the object is to project the ball against the front wall of the court in such a way that the opponent is unable to return it to the front wall in his turn before it bounces on the floor for a second time. Service is made on the full volley, while returns and all subsequent shots may be made either on the full or the half-volley. The merest whisper of a double bounce is enough to negate any shot. Service at the start of a match is decided by a spin of the racket and possession continues from the end of one game to the start of another. Only the server can score points in the trad-itional nine-point game and he continues to accrue a point per rally until deprived of ser-vice by a winning shot from his opponent, whose scoring commences from his first serve.

The server may choose to commence serving from either of the two service boxes but must thereafter serve alternately from each side. He is required to have at least one foot in contact with the floor inside the service box markings until the ball has left the strings of his racket and will be foot-faulted by the referee unless this is so, thus losing the rally.

The ball must strike the front wall above the cut line and below the out-of-court line and must fall to the floor, if allowed by the receiver, within the larger box formed by the short line and the half court line. If the ball falls outside the opposite receiving box, strikes the front, the side or the back wall above the out of court line, then the rally is lost and service is transferred.

The receiver may return the ball at any point in its flight, providing that it is not allowed to touch the floor more than once before again striking the front wall. The ball may strike either the side wall or the back wall, or both, on its way back to the front wall, but must not hit the floor between the striker's racket and the front wall. On each shot after the service the ball must strike the front wall between the out of court line at the top of the wall and the top of the tin at the bottom; the tin is strictly out of court at all times.

The simplest serve is the basic cross court volley drive at shoulder height, but this is also the easiest of balls to return even at great speed. Later we discuss the serve in detail and the techniques by which the outer limits of the court can be utilized to make returns at least more difficult and at most almost

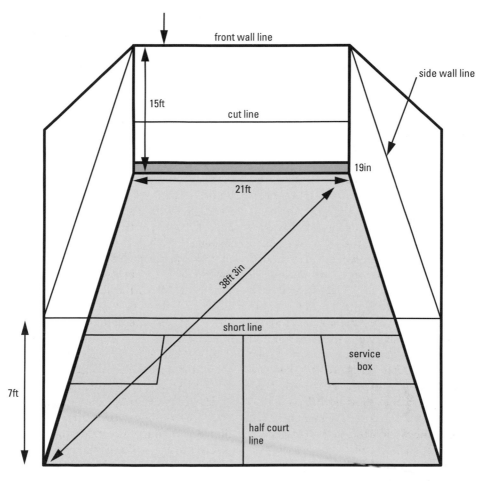

Fig 1 The court.

impossible. Similarly the simplest form of rallying is merely to strike the ball back into court within the limits discussed above, and from this a satisfying release of energy can be achieved. Below we discuss the technique that may be applied through the racket and its strings to enlarge upon the basic drive to create a wide range of variations to define, disguise and delay shots to create the space into which winners can be delivered. But first let us look at the basic elements of play.

THE GRIP

It is crucial that a beginner's first lesson should start with teaching the correct grip. In golf this is common practice, but in squash some coaches shy away from this because it takes patience and practice to master. Unlike golf, where it is almost impossible to hit the ball without the correct grip, with an eye for the ball it is easy to go on to the court, have fun and play squash. Some short-term

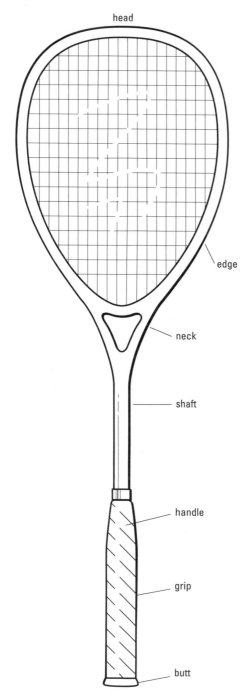

Fig 2 The racket.

success may also be achieved, but this does not translate into any long-term improvement.

If the grip is incorrect then every other aspect of the game – swing, technique, positioning, and movement – will be compromised. A correct grip dictates the angles that give one player accuracy and discipline of movement over another. In time, the right grip ensures almost total control, enabling the player to place the ball with accuracy rather than to display the mere brute force that promotes a premature tiredness.

As in other pursuits, bad habits learned early are hard to correct later on, and so it is up to coach and the student to deal with the grip properly. It is imperative that a coach does not collaborate in a pupil's natural tendency to hold the racket like a club, even if, initially, this provides good contact with the ball. To enjoy this game to the full, a firm, technical foundation is vital. It enables the pupil to reach his or her full potential and stops a falling away from the game after a couple of years through the frustration that may arise if improvement becomes elusive.

The Basic Grip

The grip must be 'open' to create an open racket face (*see* Fig 3) and the racket must be held comfortably in the fingers. A gap should remain between the first and the second finger to give manoeuvrability and control of the racket head. Ensure that the skin or the 'webbing' between the thumb and the index finger is not touching the racket handle (*see* Fig 4). Just as a top-class darts player would caress the dart rather than squeeze it, you must, when holding the racket, make sure that the grip is not held too tightly but forms more a 'cupping' action to keep the racket handle in the fingers. Also ensure that the width of a little finger is able to be placed between the palm of the hand and the racket handle itself (*see* Fig 5).

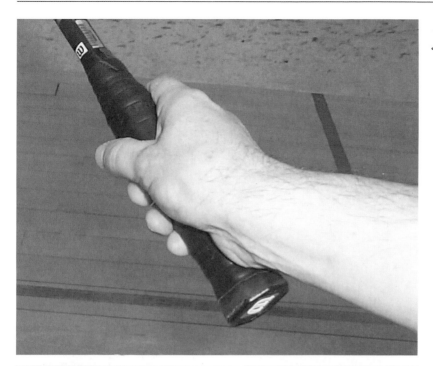

Fig 3 The correct grip.

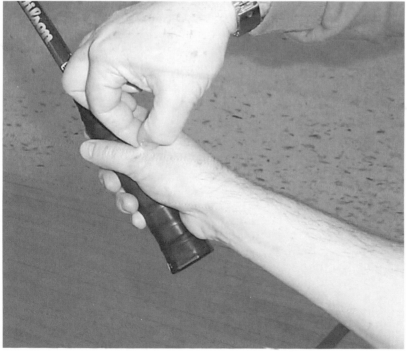

Fig 4 Pinch up the web of skin.

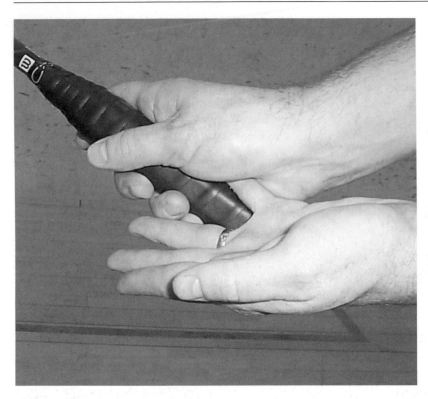

Fig 5 Space for a little finger.

What does the open grip achieve? An open grip achieves the correct angle in the preparation of the swing, leading to the correct downward motion. At impact there is an open racket face leading to the correct follow-through, which, in turn, leads to smooth movement throughout the whole stroke.

A good way to check the grip is to drop the wrist so that the butt of the racket is allowed to pass the wrist on the outside. If the grip is not right, the butt will touch the underside of the wrist (*see* Fig 6). Remember that the grip must be held lightly to create relaxation in the swing and movement. An incorrect grip leads to overcompensation and a breakdown in technique.

- Do not hold the racket in the full palm of the hand: this causes a 'frying pan' effect, full control of the ball is lost and may result in the ball hitting the tin (*see* Fig 7).
- Do not squeeze the racket handle tightly: this causes tension throughout the body and feeling is lost, thus forfeiting any touch shots such as drop shots.
- Do not let the 'webbing' between thumb and forefinger touch the handle: if the webbing is touching it is a good indicator that the racket is being held too tightly.

If there is no gap between the forefinger and the second finger maximum control of the racket head is lost.

THE MODERN SWING

Over the years the coaching method on the basic swing has remained largely unchanged. We might think of this as wooden-racket

Fig 6 Racket butt behind the wrist.

coaching, recalling days when squash rackets had small, round faces and were made mostly of wood. As racket technology advanced and the carbon-fibre graphite racket became commonplace, coaching techniques remained comfortably in a rut. While there is no doubt that some of the wooden-racket coaching methods remain valid, certain areas of the swing have moved on dramatically, due to the lightness and strength of the new type of racket. A thinner, lighter racket travels through the air quicker. This necessitates a faster response, alert reactions and a sharper, more explosive swing. This should dictate a review of coaching techniques. Furthermore, while most people easily recognize that the racket has changed, there is less recognition of how the ball itself has also changed. It is now slower and has a different weight and rubber composition. Now the ball is slower the game is less about rallying just up and down the wall and is more attacking, using all four corners of the court. Aggressive volleying is more frequent. In short, the rallies are shorter and the game is more exciting. Racket string technology has kept pace with the improved rackets. New strings now last longer and have been made specifically to suit the power of the carbon-fibre graphite racket, enabling the player to hit a crisper ball.

Coaching terminology has to change. Older coaching manuals refer often to a 'cocked wrist' when describing the swing and this is still widely taught. A more suitable

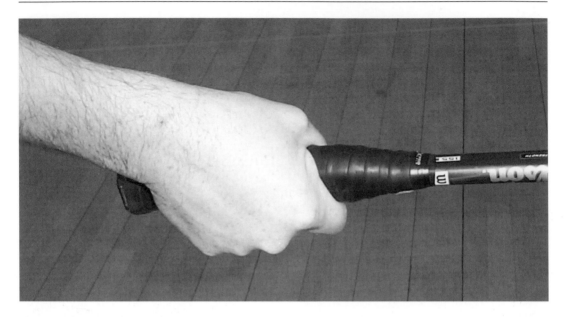

Fig 7 Forbidden frying pan effect.

description of the wrist in the modern swing is firm but relaxed. The wrist is no longer cocked, removing the tension that results from it, enabling the player to really 'throw' into the swing. It is hoped that this book will bring up to date for the first time the methods used currently by England's world-class coaching team; these are the techniques used by the top English international players.

THE BASIC SWING

Spacing

This is the area that creates the correct distance between the racket and the body. The resting point is at waist height, with the racket head towards the side wall. The first movement of the racket should be away from the body, towards the side wall and then into the swing by raising the shoulder. Many people would simply use the arm but it is

Fig 8 The rest position.

important that this movement stems from the shoulder, gradually raising the racket in rhythm with the ball. The hips and the chest will start to turn towards the back corner with a relaxed grip and lots of spacing under the arm and away from the body. The aim is to create space in the highlighted area. By this movement, the correct momentum will have been built up to deliver the swing into the ball.

The Delivery of the Swing

The racket will now be held lightly in the fingers ready to throw the racket head from the shoulder. Just before the swing breaks, the racket head should be pointing to the ceiling. The shoulder and the grip should be relaxed.

The Initial Break of the Swing

By rotating the shoulder, the racket head will drop behind the body. This movement will naturally take the racket head towards the opposite side wall. The elbow will now be turned into the body, roughly level with the waist. At this point the racket will be poised at the correct angle, the racket edge ready to cut cleanly through the air.

The Extension of the Elbow and the Wrist

The racket head must travel slightly behind the wrist. The elbow extends and locks. The

Fig 9 Low shoulder.

Fig 10 High shoulder.

Fig 11 Create space for the shot.

Fig 12 Racket hand towards ceiling.

power created by the elbow throws the wrist and the racket head to impact with the ball.

Impact

The racket face should be open on impact with the ball. This creates side-spin due to the sharp angle of the swing (*see* Fig 15). The point of impact will now be away from the body, with the elbow extended and in line with the leading leg.

Rotation of the Forearm

Immediately after impact, the forearm will rotate and the racket head should be 'thrown'

towards the corner of the court where the side wall meets the front wall.

Full Extension of the Shoulder

After the rotation of the forearm and the racket has been thrown, the shoulder must be extended. This enables the player to sustain the correct pathway to the corner of the court, keeping the racket away from the chest into a full completion of the follow-through.

Recoil

Correct recoil of the racket head happens only if the elbow, the wrist and the shoulder are

Fig 13 A clean cutting edge.

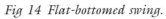

Fig 14 Flat-bottomed swing.

Fig 15 Full arm extension at impact.

Fig 16 Racket head thrown towards corner.

Fig 17 Follow through completely.

Fig 18 Recoil back to rest position.

Fig 19 Rest position.

at full extension. The power created by this action achieves the correct recoil with the arm and shoulder acting as a spring to pull the player back to the 'T' position in one fluid movement.

Resting Position

The resting position evolves from the recoil action and leaves the racket at waist height, ready for the next shot.

BASIC FOOTWORK AND MOVEMENT

When moving towards the ball from the 'T', the weight is transferred on to the back leg ready to strike the ball. Transfer some of the weight from this leg on to the leading leg in one natural rhythm so that the swing and

Fig 20 (ABOVE AND LEFT) Weight from back to front foot forehand.

movement are fluid and as one. It is important that this is not two separate movements
since this will interrupt the rhythm of them.
Note that the back leg on the left-handed
forehand is the left leg. The leading leg, on
to which weight will be transferred, will be
the right leg. The opposite occurs on the
backhand and, of course, everything is
reversed for a right-hander.

At all times movement must be in rhythm
with the ball so that movement and swing
are as one to give the correct relaxed, smooth
and economical style. This is important both
to conserve energy and to prevent tiredness.

Notes

1. Bellamy, R., *Squash: A History* (Heinemann
   Kingswood, 1987).

*Fig 21 (RIGHT AND BELOW) Weight from
back to front foot backhand.*

CHAPTER 2

The Life Game

Squash is not a game to be taken up and left off like a favourite sweater. It necessarily becomes part of the player's life; room must be made for it to a greater or lesser degree in busy schedules and patterns of living must be shaped to take account of its demands. If this seems an extreme suggestion, just talk to even the most ordinary, regular player who drops out of the game for a while, either through injury or time demands elsewhere, about how difficult it is to get squash back into a diary which seems magically to have expanded to fill all the court times that previously existed harmoniously with other activities.

Here we examine how players of a variety of standards and commitment can maximize their dedication to the game.

SOCIAL PLAYERS

At the grass-roots level of the game many players enjoy a couple of sessions a week just for the run and the fun of friendly competition. But such is the nature of squash and its unusual physical demands, that it is as well to approach even this usually escalating social involvement with some care. Even if you are trying the game for the first time, perhaps taking it up because you have noticed others on the courts as you walk to and from the gymnasium and you are still wearing your string vest, you still need to do a little more preparation than merely turning your baseball cap back to front. Your body, after all, is just as important to you as the finely honed version is to even the highest paid professional.

Dehydration is an aspect of physical well-being all too often ignored even in normal day-to-day life. Medical opinion suggests that a minimum of 2 litres (about 3½ pints) of water a day is essential. Half a litre taken an hour before play and another soon after finishing the match can work wonders with energy levels both during and after the activity. It is worth restraining the urge for a plunge into social drinking immediately after play. Nothing dehydrates the body as fast as alcohol. Have another pint of water, perhaps flavoured with fruit juice or one of the sports isotonic additives, before you think of drinking beer or spirits.

Some of the advice given later here for more advanced players can only be beneficial even at the social level, but stretching and warming-up (and warming-down) are in some ways even more important to the occasional player than to the high-level performer. The squash court is not a controlled environment. Explosive movement and sustained effort affect heart rate, pulse rate and muscle condition. In the untutored physique these may wreak havoc from which long-term damage can result and, at the very least, enthusiasm for the game can be dimmed. Five to ten minutes immediately before stepping on to the court and immediately after the end of a match, following the sort of programme discussed in Chapter 7, are all it takes to soften the muscles in anticipation of action and run them down to a resting state afterwards. This habit is like having money in the bank for the next match.

CLUB LEAGUE PLAYERS

Anyone with even a passing interest in club league competition is going to be on court three or four times a week at least, so during the season there is not a great call for background training, although you might care to look at the advice on summer work that we suggest for more involved players.

It is possible, however, for a keen league player to improve his or her fitness by extending the stretching and warming-up or warming-down into mini-fitness sessions. Before the match, stretching and warming as advised in Chapter 7 are the best entry to activity. After the match, a ten-minute session, probably on another court away from the competitive action, perhaps involving five sets of twenty court sprints one time, or a long, rhythmic, ghosting session (ball-less practice) at another, or explosive ghosting, or visualization ghosting – in which you imagine playing against the strengths and weaknesses of a closely matched opponent – can build your fitness and resources steadily beyond what is required of you in actual match play. It is also a hard thing for your opponents to watch, especially if you have just beaten them, and that is valuable psychology in the bank for the next time you meet them. After this compressed work-out, stretching and warming-down become even more important.

Jansher Khan's favourite trick at the end of a fairly easy, early-round match was to invite any player in the club to step on court

for nine points. Often there would be a long line of hopefuls outside his court while the tournament continued. By the end of the evening his upcoming opponents would hear nothing except tales of Jansher's incredible prowess and stamina. Guess what they were thinking about when they closed the door to start their own encounter with the master?

A league player needs to be more targeted towards an upcoming match than a social player. During the day preceding a league confrontation the minimum quantity of water prescribed earlier should be taken: that is plain water or water with fruit juice or isotonic additives, not the usual tea or coffee that act differently on the body chemistry. Eating should also be thoughtfully controlled through the day: a reasonable breakfast is required but lunch should be light, perhaps only pasta and sweetcorn, and only snacks such as power bars or healthy sandwiches should be consumed for the rest of the day, and not in the quantities to make up for the lack of a big meal nor too close to match time. No alcohol at all should be drunk on the day of the match, but the same amount of water both before and after the match as was indicated above.

TEAM PLAYERS

League players who move on to represent a club in district leagues and similar competitions must take on board everything suggested for league players and must certainly be thinking of building a summer base-training schedule into their lives and take training from a recognized Level 4 coach for shot production, tactics and shot selection.

This player will be on court almost every day, with background training aimed towards three-month cycles incorporating power and endurance work. Some friendly matches, perhaps with team colleagues, should be designed to incorporate pairs training and pyramid training as discussed in Chapter 7 and every playing session should be followed by the sort of ten-minute sessions suggested for league players.

On match days, as far as working life allows, the main emphasis should be on the approaching confrontation and lunch should be preceded by a half-hour solo session, preferably on a court as similar as possible to the one reserved for the match play. Paul Carter suggests the following routine as an ideal solo practice lasting about 50 minutes normally but cut back to about half-an-hour on match days:

Fig 22 Paul Carter working solo.

1. 150 drives to length forehand using four floorboards as target width
2. 25 drops forehand in the front court, using free hand to throw the ball
3. 150 drives to length backhand using four floorboards as target width
4. 25 drops backhand in the front court, using free hand to throw the ball
5. 100 volleys to length, forehand side middle/back of box, letting the occasional ball go to the back wall to check length
6. 25 drops to mid-court forehand, self-feeding off front wall
7. 100 volleys to length, backhand side middle/back of box, letting the occasional ball go to the back wall to check length
8. 25 drops to mid-court backhand, self-feeding off the front wall
9. 75 straight volley drop kills, varying feed in front of forehand box
10. 75 straight volley drop kills, varying feed in front of backhand box
11. 25 cross-court kills forehand, in front of box
12. 25 cross-court kills backhand, in front of box
13. 200 figure-of-eight half-volleys
14. 20 serves on each hand.

The aim should be to search for quality throughout the exercise.

Arrival at the playing venue should be arranged to ensure at least an hour before court time in order to take care of unexpected problems, deal with team matters, drink enough water early enough and think about the match. Good relations with the rest of the club squad, not just the captain because he makes the selection and ranking decisions, are basic to team performance. Of course, some personalities just do not click together and the best way to deal with this is for them to stay out of each other's way, especially during and around each other's matches. But there is nothing to say that you cannot fetch water to the court for your not-so-favourite team-mate, or get a wrist band or chase up a missing referee. Some players like to be left completely alone during their matches, others need corner work between games. A team will work out who is best in whose corner, but, if matches clash, you have to know enough about everyone's game plan, its strengths and weaknesses, to be able to step into the corner for any member of the team. Remember, though, corner work is not about popping in at the end of each game to hold the racket and exchange pleasantries. You need at least to keep an eye on what is happening on court. You need to be able to offer either encouragement about what your player is doing successfully or to suggest the means of improvement.

Most players do not take in much in the 90sec break. Concentrate on injecting the single most important comment you have on what you have seen, then do the chores, the water, the racket, the grip, the towel, even the place to sit down, while your player absorbs your comment and thinks about what to do next. If friendship and trust already exist between you, simply being there might be enough to push home that vital game that spells the difference between victory and defeat at the end of the night, even at the end of the season.

NATIONAL-LEVEL PLAYERS

Lifting one's performance from the club intra-county level to the national inter-county level is the great step change from 'amateur' to 'professional' thinking in squash. The process may last two or three years, and, given the premise that you have sufficient talent in the first place, coaching is probably 75 per cent of the task.

It is time to reach for the sports science knowledge that has accumulated over the past decade or so. The Squash Rackets Association (SRA) now lists coaches who are qualified in modern techniques and at this level players should be casting around their local area for at least Level 4 coaches to whom they can connect on a continuing basis. It is no longer good enough to learn from your peers or to spend time with the good player at your club from whom you might have learnt so much. Your coach should be putting you in touch with the scientific specialities and moving you into areas of technical expertise beyond your previous knowledge.

This is the time to start tuning into physiological expertise that will design the summer training that is to become the base platform of your performance, with personalized top-up programmes during the season. The workload will increase so much at this level that stretching will become a daily chore of at least an hour's duration. It need not intrude on other things, you can stretch while watching television, conversing or doing household chores. Psychology is also a valuable tool at this level. You will want to set your targets for each season and be able to assess your progress. You will want to inspect your weaknesses and strengths in a balanced context and with someone you trust who understands exactly how you are progressing. Together you will enter the politics of competition: the player you have to beat to get into the county side, for instance, and what record of achievement must be assembled to penetrate a particular arena.

During this extended process you will begin to tap into individual tournaments. Graded tournaments are becoming an increasing part of the domestic scene and there are varying levels of competition to approach. In some events you might be among the leading contenders, in others you will be doing well at first to get out of the qualifiers or the first round. All the time you will be getting used to the rigours of travelling, of sleeping in strange beds and of playing in unfamiliar environments against unknown opponents. You will be gathering experience of dealing with all this alone, with only your increasing knowledge and your personal experience to rely upon in most instances.

PROFESSIONAL PLAYERS

If all goes well at the national level, the thought will arise that life as a professional squash player might be worth at least a trial. This is the point at which the step change to professionalism must be completed. Instead of fitting your squash into normal civil life, you will need to make the game the centre of your being, with normal life being fitted around the demands of your new 'job'.

All that has been discussed previously is incorporated into this existence. There will be carefully designed, summer base training, scientific input to the planning of technical training, physical condition and psychology. You will probably be seeking the best specialists in each field that might be available. No professional has ever succeeded at the top of this game without this sort of input, at least in the early years, and never has such good scientific help been so readily available.

On days that do not actually include a competitive match – and there will be fewer of them the higher you rise – you will come to see the daylight hours as the working day in the same way as a banker, builder, taxi-driver or shop assistant does. You do not lie abed simply because you are now 'professional' and self-employed. Rising around 9am, taking a light breakfast of cereal, fruit and tea, you will be at the court by 10am for a half hour of stretching, while taking on board the usual quantity of water, checking kit and sorting rackets, shoes and towels. Around 10.30 you should be ready to go on court, with or without a coach, working on the fine tuning of technique, shots and movement, with a hard pressure session of about half an hour, followed by stretching and warming-down.

A two- or three-hours lunch break will include a meal, probably of pasta or something similar, and time spent on administration, domestic chores and such like. Remember that a large part of early professional life is the simple organizing of time and expenses. You will be running your home life, like anyone else, but you will also be arranging entries, booking flights, making sure of accommodation and attending to what you hope will be a growing diary of publicity and promotional events.

At about 3pm you will be back at the coal-face, stretching for half an hour in anticipation of a demanding best-of-five with one of your training partners (perhaps a member of your training camp or another independent operator like yourself). You will probably be trying to put into competitive action some of the points you worked on in the day's earlier session. You might put a video camera behind the court on some days so that, warming-down and stretching, you can have ten minutes of analysis either on your own or with your coach.

On days when you are still travel-stained or flight-weary, the hard five-setter might be better replaced by solo ghosting, lengths or strengths, but still a camera and analysis can be brought into play as the basis for discussion about your progress and development with your coach. Evenings on these non-match days should be spent as with 'civilians' – with your family, at the cinema, the club or watching television.

On match days things take a different shape. Assuming that there is a match for around 5pm the professional would rise at his customary time and breakfast in the usual way, on cereal and fruit, most probably bananas. He would then go to the venue for the match and preferably to the court that he was likely to play on later. There he would practise solo or with a feed from the coach for 30 to 40min only, with a half-hour light massage afterwards.

Light personal chores could follow, with lunch being taken three to four hours before the scheduled match time. Pasta or a baked potato with a tasty topping would be ideal.

Lots of water and snacks, power bars or bananas should also be taken two or three times during the day. After lunch comes the siesta, preferably waking a couple of hours before match time, and then a relaxed return to the venue an hour or so before the action is due to start to allow time for stretching and mental preparation.

All of this can be adjusted up or down according to the actual match time; usually some flexibility and patience will be required in order to take in delays caused by previous matches being extended beyond their expected end.

CHAPTER 3

The Technical Game

The aim of this chapter is to introduce the modern way of coaching and playing and to pose questions about the preconceived ideas that have been passed down over the generations. It is vital to remember that, as with all sports, the environment that squash is played in is ever changing. Arguably, most documented squash techniques would not endure the increasing demands of the modern game. What we are trying to deliver is the excitement and aggression that exists in the modern game, which is being used by the top England players with great success. The following techniques can be employed by players of all standards, from the beginner to the world's top players.

THE FOREHAND DRIVE

Preparation

When approaching the ball from the 'T' you must make sure that your body is round on the ball so that you are in a position to use the correct technique to deliver the racket at the correct angle. The position you are in now should allow you to deliver the preparation stage with the techniques outlined in Chapter 1. On the forehand you can hit the ball off either leg.

Points to Remember
- Correct grip.
- First movement of the racket head is away from the body towards the side wall.

- Let the racket bring the left shoulder round, with your chest almost facing the ball wall.
- As the racket rises, make sure that your weight is being transferred on to the back leg (like a baseball pitcher).
- On impact, weight should be evenly distributed through the body from back to front.
- Do not allow weight to take you through the ball (falling through the shot).

Fig 23 Weight transfers to back leg as racket rises.

Delivery

You are now at the delivery stage of the swing into the ball (remember: no cocked wrist). You want to release the racket head to come from a high position so that it is ready to cut down into the ball. You must make sure that the racket head is then laid back into a flat-bottomed swing. Let the leading edge of the racket cut into the ball with the swing constantly gaining speed. At impact a lot of sidespin is imparted on the ball. This action is created by the elbow extending and the wrist is released to produce power at the last split second.

Follow-Through

All the above-mentioned points are vital to a good delivery; however, the follow-through is the part of the swing that most players

Fig 24 Laying back the racket head, forehand.

Fig 25 Extending the elbow at forehand impact.

tend to ignore. If you do not use the follow-through correctly the preparation and the delivery break down. The follow-through is of immense importance as it controls the rhythm of the swing. The extension of the shoulder will automatically create the space required at the end of the follow-through, with the racket head finishing in a high position. The power that has been created through preparation, delivery and follow-through is known as the recoil effect. This allows you keep control of your balance through the shot and helps the recovery movement.

Common Mistakes to Avoid

Preparation
Do not tuck the elbow into the body
Do not keep the shoulders square on to the side wall
Do not grip the racket too tightly
Do not cock the wrist

Delivery of Swing
Do not use the 'U'-shape swing
Do not over rotate at the waist, forcing your chest to face the front wall
Do not hit the ball with the flat face ('frying pan')

Follow-Through
Do not go under the non-playing arm
Do not finish low on the follow-through

Deep from the Back Corners

The same principles apply as with the straight forehand drive, apart from hitting under the ball with an open racket face, aiming higher on the front wall. The body must be lower, with bent knees. The extension of the follow-through is a little higher; this also helps you rhythmically to move back to your 'T' position.

Fig 26 High finish on forehand follow-through.

THE BACKHAND DRIVE

Preparation

Follow the guidance given for the straight forehand drive. On the backhand side the leading leg should generally be the right leg.

Points to Remember
- Correct grip.
- First movement of the racket head is away from the body towards the side wall.
- Drop the forearm, turning the shoulder, which in turn pulls the hip around.

31

- As the racket rises, make sure that your weight is being transferred on to the back leg (baseball pitcher).
- The racket should rise in rhythm with the ball, making sure that you lift your shoulder; the elbow should break only at this point, not before.
- On impact, the weight should be evenly distributed through the body from back to front.

- Do not allow the weight to take you through the ball (falling through the shot).

Delivery

Follow the guidance given for the straight forehand drive.

Follow-Through

Follow the guidance given for the straight forehand drive.

Fig 27 Shoulder turning into high backhand preparation.

Fig 28 Flat-bottomed swing on back-hand.

Fig 29 Elbow extending into backhand wrist release.

Common Mistakes to Avoid

Preparation
Do not break the elbow straightaway
Do not tuck the elbow into the body
Do not grip the racket too tightly
Do not cock the wrist
Do not break the wrist on impact
Delivery of Swing
Do not use the 'U'-shape swing
Do not hit the ball with the flat face
Follow-Through
Do not finish low on the follow-through
Do not finish the follow through on the opposite side of the body

Deep from the Back Corners

Follow the guidance given for the straight forehand drive.

Fig 30 Relaxing into recoil to 'T'.

FOREHAND CROSS-COURT DRIVE

Preparation

Follow the guidance given for the straight forehand drive. On the forehand you can hit the ball off either leg.

Points to Remember
- Correct grip.
- First movement of the racket head is away from the body towards the side wall.
- As the racket rises, make sure that your weight is being transferred on to the back leg (baseball pitcher).
- The racket should rise in rhythm with the ball, making sure that you lift your shoulder; the elbow should break only at this point, not before.

Fig 31 Approaching the ball for forehand cross.

Fig 32 Cutting across the ball.

Things Not to Do
- Do not turn shoulders to face the back wall.
- Do not tuck the elbow into the body.
- Do not grip the racket too tightly.
- Do not cock the wrist.
- Do not take the ball behind your leading leg.

Delivery

The delivery stage is the same as with the forehand straight drive. The only difference is the scything action at impact cutting across the ball.

Points to Remember
- Take the ball slightly in front of the leading leg; the chest should be facing the side.
- Throw the edge of the racket from the flat-bottomed swing in a scything motion, cutting across the ball.
- On impact, the weight should be evenly distributed through the body from back to front.

Things Not to Do
- Do not use the 'U'-shape swing.
- Do not hit the ball with the flat face.

Follow-Through

The follow-through is virtually the same as the straight drive; the only difference being that it finishes across the body.

Fig 33 Elbow extending fully for cross-court forehand.

Fig 34 Pointing the racket at the wall on cross-court follow-through.

Points to Remember
- After impact, release your non-playing arm to make way for the follow-through.
- Do not allow your weight to take you through the ball (falling through the shot).
- The follow-through is to finish high with a rotation of the forearm towards the opposite side wall.
- The follow-through will help to turn the body so you can recover to the 'T' position.

Things Not to Do
- Do not finish low on the follow-through.
- Do not finish the follow-through on the opposite side of the body.
- Do not turn the body at the same time as when the follow-through is taking place.

Deep from the Back Corners

The same principles apply as with the straight forehand drive.

THE BACKHAND CROSS-COURT DRIVE

Preparation

Follow the guidance given for the forehand drive. On the forehand you can hit the ball off either leg.

Points to Remember
- Correct grip.
- First movement of the racket head is away from the body towards the side wall.
- As the racket rises make sure that your weight is being transferred on to the back leg (baseball pitcher).
- Drop the forearm, turning the shoulder, which in turn pulls the hip around.

- The racket should rise in rhythm with the ball, making sure that you lift your shoulder; the elbow should break only at this point, not before.

Things Not to Do
- Do not turn shoulders to face the back wall.
- Do not tuck the elbow into the body.
- Do not grip the racket too tightly.
- Do not cock the wrist.
- Do not take the ball behind your leading leg.

Fig 35 Turning shoulder and dropping forearm on cross-court backhand.

Delivery

The delivery stage is the same as with the forehand cross-court drive; the only difference is the scything action at impact cutting across the ball.

Points to Remember

- Take the ball slightly in front of the leading leg; the chest should be facing the side. Throw the edge of the racket from the flat-bottomed swing in a scything motion, cutting across the ball.
- On impact, the weight should be evenly distributed through the body from back to front.

Fig 36 Racket and shoulder rising in rhythm.

Things Not to Do

- Do not use the 'U'-shape swing.
- Do not hit the ball with the flat face.

Follow-Through

The follow-through is virtually the same as in the straight drive; the only difference is that it finishes across the body.

Points to Remember

- After impact, release your non-playing arm to make way for the follow-through.
- Do not allow your weight to take you through the ball (falling through the shot).
- The follow-through is to finish high, with a rotation of the forearm towards the opposite side wall.
- The follow-through will help to turn the body so you can recover to the 'T' position.

Fig 37 Scything racket face across the ball.

Things Not to Do
- Do not finish low on the follow-through.
- Do not finish the follow-through on the opposite side of the body.
- Do not turn the body at the same time as the follow-through is taking place.

Deep from the Back Corners

The same principles apply as in the straight backhand drive.

Fig 38 *Follow-through helps you back to the 'T'.*

THE FOREHAND DROP SHOT

Preparation

Follow the guidance given for the straight forehand drive. On the forehand you can hit the ball off either leg.

Points to Remember
- Correct grip.
- A slight movement of the racket head away from the body towards the side wall.
- There should be lots of space under the arm, with the elbow away from the body.
- The preparation is not as high as with the drive.
- A gentle pick up of the racket head which should be in rhythm with the pace of the ball.

Fig 39 *Shoulder round and racket lower than straight forehand.*

Fig 40 Open racket face at full extension.

Things Not to Do
- Do not raise the racket too high unless the ball is sitting up.
- Do not cock the wrist and have the elbow too tight to the body.
- Do not grip the racket too tightly.
- Do not have an excessive swing.

Delivery

Points to Remember
- The racket head is laid back into the flat-bottom swing coming into the ball with the leading edge.
- The racket and arm is out in front of the opponent.
- Release the elbow and wrist with extension of the forearm.
- The racket head should be open and in a slight downward position.
- Strike the ball on the inside in order to impart side spin.
- Strike the ball in front of your leading leg.

Things Not to Do
- Do not have a closed face at impact.
- Do not jab at the ball; feel the ball on to the strings.
- Do not hit the ball too hard.
- Do not hold the grip with too much tension.

Follow-Through

Points to Remember
- A gentle follow-through with an extension of the shoulder to direct and feel the ball.
- At the end of the follow-through a gentle recoil to help you recover off the shot.

Things Not to Do
- Do not be too quick with the follow-through.
- Do not quit on the follow-through (relax).
- Do not keep the elbow bent.

Fig 41 Gentle follow-through.

Fig 42 Recoil recovery to 'T'.

THE BACKHAND DROP SHOT

Preparation

Follow the guidance given for the forehand drive. On the backhand you want to hit the ball off the right leg.

Points to Remember
- Correct grip.
- A slight movement of the racket head away from the body towards the side wall.
- There should be lots of space under the arm, with the elbow away from the body.
- The preparation is not as high as with the drive.
- A gentle pick up of the racket head, which should be in rhythm with the pace of the ball.

Things Not to Do
- Do not raise the racket too high unless the ball is sitting up.
- Do not cock the wrist and have the elbow too tight to the body.
- Do not grip the racket too tightly.
- Do not have an excessive swing.

Delivery

Points to Remember
- The racket head is laid back into the flat-bottom swing, coming into the ball with the leading edge.
- The racket and arm are out in front of the opponent.
- Release the elbow and wrist with extension of the forearm.

Fig 43 Correct approach angle.

Fig 44 Racket head open in downward direction.

Fig 45 Striking the ball in front of lead leg.

Fig 46 Recoil to rest position at 'T'.

- The racket head should be open and in a slightly downward position.
- You are still striking the ball on the inside, but you can use more side spin; you can drop the elbow steeply, but without breaking the wrist.
- The racket head may be lower than on the forehand side.
- Strike the ball in front of your leading leg.

Things Not to Do
- Do not have a closed face at impact.
- Do not jab at the ball; feel the ball on to the strings.
- Do not hit the ball too hard.
- Do not hold the grip with too much tension.

Follow-Through

Points to Remember
- A gentle follow-through with an extension of the shoulder to direct and feel the ball.
- At the end of the follow-through, a gentle recoil to help you to recover off the shot.

Things Not to Do
- Do not be too quick with the follow-through.
- Do not quit on the follow-through (relax).
- Do not keep the elbow bent.

THE FOREHAND VOLLEY

Preparation

Follow the guidance given for the forehand drive. On the forehand you may hit the ball off either leg.

Points to Remember
- Correct grip.
- A slight movement of the racket head away from the body towards the side wall.

Fig 47 Shoulder round on early forehand volley preparation.

- As the rackets rises, make sure that your weight is being transferred on to the back leg (baseball pitcher).
- Let the racket bring the shoulder round with your chest facing the back wall.
- Raise the racket up to shoulder height.
- Make sure your body weight is rising up into the delivery.
- There should be lots of space under the arm, with the elbow away from the body.

Things Not to Do
- Do not allow your weight to take you through the ball (falling through the shot).
- Do not cock the wrist and have the elbow too tight to the body.
- Do not grip the racket too tightly.
- Do not have an excessive swing.

Fig 48 Laying the face open to the ceiling at shoulder height.

Fig 49 Elbow and wrist extended with open face.

Delivery

Points to Remember
- The racket head is laid back into the flat-bottom swing, coming into the ball with the leading edge.
- The racket and arm are out in front of the opponent.
- Release the elbow and wrist, with extension of the forearm; the racket head is released in a punching action like a boxer delivering a jab.
- Take the ball in line with the non-playing shoulder with an open racket face.

Things Not to Do
- Do not have a closed face at impact.
- Do not hold the grip with too much tension.

Follow-Through

Points to Remember and Things Not to Do
- As with the forehand drive.

Fig 50 Relax into recoil to 'T'.

THE BACKHAND VOLLEY

Preparation

Follow the guidance given for the forehand drive. On the backhand you should hit the ball off the right leg.

Points to Remember
- Correct grip.
- The first movement of the racket head is away from the body towards the side wall.

Fig 51 Shoulder round on early backhand volley preparation.

- Drop the forearm, turning the shoulder, which, in turn, pulls the hip around.
- As the racket rises make sure your weight is being transferred on to the back leg.
- Raise the racket up to shoulder height.
- Make sure your body weight is rising up into the delivery.
- There should be lots of space under the arm, with the elbow away from the body.

Things Not to Do
- Do not cock the wrist and have the elbow too tight to the body.
- Do not grip the racket too tightly.
- Do not have an excessive swing.

Delivery
Points to Remember
- The racket head is laid back into the flat bottom swing, coming into the ball with the leading edge.
- The racket and arm are out in front of the opponent.
- Release the elbow and wrist; with extension of the forearm, the racket head is released in a punching action.
- Take the ball in line with the playing shoulder with an open racket face.

Things Not to Do
- Do not have a closed face at impact.
- Do not hold the grip with too much tension.

Fig 52 Laying the face open to the ceiling at shoulder height.

Fig 53 Elbow and wrist extended with open face.

Fig 54 Relax into recoil to 'T'.

Follow-Through

Points to Remember and Things Not to Do
- As with the backhand drive.

THE FOREHAND VOLLEY DROP

Preparation

Follow the guidance given for the forehand drive. On the forehand you can hit the ball off either leg.

Points to Remember
- Correct grip.
- A slight movement of the racket head away from the body towards the side wall, at shoulder height.

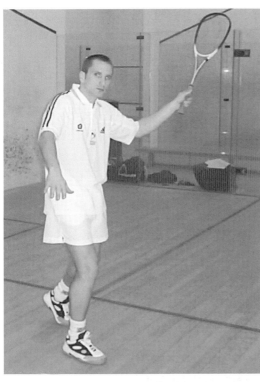

- There should be plenty of space under the arm, with the elbow away from the body.
- A gentle pick-up of the racket head, which should be in rhythm with the pace of the ball.

Things Not to Do
- Do not raise the racket too high unless the ball is sitting up.
- Do not cock the wrist and have the elbow too tight to the body.
- Do not grip the racket too tightly.
- Do not have an excessive swing.

Delivery

Points to Remember
- The racket head is laid back into the flat bottom swing, coming into the ball with the leading edge.
- The racket and arm are out in front of the opponent.

Fig 55 (ABOVE LEFT) Making space under the arm on forehand volley drop.

Fig 56 (LEFT) Racket head open and descending.

Fig 57 Strike ball in front of lead leg.

Fig 58 Recoil to rest position at 'T'.

- Release the elbow and wrist, with extension of the forearm.
- The racket head should be open and in a slightly downward position.
- Strike the ball on the inside in order to impart side spin.
- Strike the ball in front of your leading leg.

Things Not to Do
- Do not have a closed face at impact.
- Do not jab at the ball, feel the ball on to the strings.
- Do not hit the ball too hard.
- Do not hold the grip with too much tension.

Follow-Through

Points to Remember
- A gentle follow-through with an extension of the shoulder to direct and feel the ball.
- At the end of the follow-through, a gentle recoil to help you recover off the shot.

Things Not to Do
- Do not be too quick with the follow-through.
- Do not quit on the follow-through but relax.
- Do not keep the elbow bent.

THE BACKHAND VOLLEY DROP

Preparation

Follow the guidance given for the forehand drive. On the backhand you want to hit the ball off the right leg.

Fig 59 Bring the body round on the ball for backhand volley drop.

Points to Remember
- Correct grip.
- A slight movement of the racket head away from the body towards the side wall.
- There should be plenty of space under the arm, with the elbow away from the body, at shoulder height.
- A gentle pick-up of the racket head, which should be in rhythm with the pace of the ball.

Things Not to Do
- Do not raise the racket too high unless the ball is sitting up.
- Do not cock the wrist and have the elbow too tight to the body.
- Do not grip the racket too tightly.
- Do not have an excessive swing.

Delivery

Points to Remember
- The racket head is laid back into the flat bottom swing, coming into the ball with the leading edge.
- The racket and arm are out in front of the opponent.
- Release the elbow and wrist with extension of the forearm.
- The racket head should be open and in a slightly downward position.
- You are still striking the ball on the inside, but you may use more side spin.
- You may drop the elbow steeply, but without breaking the wrist.
- The racket head may be lower than on the forehand side.
- Strike the ball in front of your leading leg.
- The technique for cross-court volleys is the same as for cross-court drives, apart from the ball being taken in the air with more of a punching action.

Fig 60 Open racket edge cuts down into ball.

Fig 61 Strike without breaking the wrist.

Things Not to Do
- Do not have a closed face at impact.
- Do not jab at the ball, feel the ball on to the strings.
- Do not hit the ball too hard.
- Do not hold the grip with too much tension.

Follow-Through

Points to Remember
- A gentle follow-through with an extension of the shoulder to direct and feel the ball.
- At the end of the follow-through, a gentle recoil to help you recover off the shot.

Things Not to Do
- Do not be too quick with the follow-through.
- Do not quit on the follow-through but relax.
- Do not keep the elbow bent.

Fig 62 Recoil to rest position at 'T'.

THE FOREHAND BOAST

Preparation

Follow the guidance given for the forehand drive. On the forehand you can hit the ball off either leg.

Points to Remember
- Correct grip.
- First movement of the racket head is away from the body towards the side wall.
- Let the racket bring the left shoulder round, with your chest almost facing the ball wall.
- As the racket rises, make sure that your weight is transferred on to the back leg.
- On impact, the weight should be evenly distributed through the body from back to front.

Fig 63 Lead shoulder round towards back wall for forehand boast.

Fig 64 Laying back the racket head below wrist.

Fig 65 Striking with face open and below wrist.

Things Not to Do
- Do not tuck the elbow into the body.
- Do not keep shoulders square-on to the side wall.
- Do not grip the racket too tightly.
- Do not cock the wrist.

Delivery

You are now at the delivery stage of the swing into the ball (remember: no cocked wrist). You want to release the racket head to come from a high position so that it is ready to cut down into the ball. You must make sure that the racket head is then laid back into a flat-bottomed swing. Let the leading edge of the racket cut into the ball with the swing constantly gaining speed. At impact, a lot of sidespin is imparted to the ball. This action is created by the elbow extending; the wrist is then released to produce power at the last split second. Hit the ball into the side wall with the racket face open at impact, cutting across the ball with the racket head slightly below the wrist. The ball should then be hit slightly up the side wall, but still keeping the feet and the body facing the side wall. Remember: think of the side wall as the front wall, because whatever happens on the side wall dictates what happens when the ball reaches the front wall.

Things Not to Do
- Do not use the 'U'-shape swing.
- Do not over-rotate at the waist, forcing your chest to face the front wall.
- Do not hit the ball with the flat face.

Follow-Through

All the above-mentioned points are vital to a good delivery; however, the follow-through is the part of the swing that most players tend to ignore. If you do not use the follow-through correctly the preparation and delivery break down. The follow-through is of immense importance as it controls the rhythm of the swing. The extension of the shoulder will automatically create the space required at the end of the follow-through, with the racket head finishing in a high position. The power that has been created through preparation and delivery takes the follow-through towards the 'T' position with your weight, after impact, falling into the 'T' position. The recoil allows you keep control of your balance through the shot and helps the recovery movement.

Things Not to Do
- Do not go under the non-playing arm.
- Do not finish low on the follow-through.

Fig 66 Racket head finishes high in front of body.

THE BACKHAND BOAST

Preparation

Follow the guidance given for the forehand drive. On the backhand you should hit the ball off the right leg.

Points to Remember
- Correct grip.
- First movement of the racket head is away from the body towards the side wall.
- Let the racket bring the left shoulder round, with your chest almost facing the back wall.

- As the racket rises, make sure that your weight is transferred on to the back leg.
- On impact, the weight should be evenly distributed through the body from back to front.

Things Not to Do
- Do not tuck the elbow into the body.
- Do not keep the shoulders square-on to the side wall.
- Do not grip the racket too tightly.
- Do not cock the wrist.

Delivery

As for the forehand boast.

Fig 67 Letting the shoulder bring the racket round for backhand boast.

Fig 68 Racket head laid back for flat swing.

Fig 69 (ABOVE)
Full arm extension
with side spin.

Fig 70 (LEFT)
Follow-through
takes you to 'T'.

Things Not to Do
- Do not use the 'U'-shape swing.
- Do not over-rotate at the waist, forcing your chest to face the front wall.
- Do not hit the ball with the flat face.

Follow-Through

As for the forehand boast.

Things Not to Do
- Do not finish low on the follow-through.
- Do not finish the follow-through on the opposite side of the body.

THE FOREHAND LOB

Preparation

Follow the guidance given for the forehand drive. On the forehand you can hit the ball off either leg.

Points to Remember
- Correct grip.
- A slight movement of the racket head away from the body towards the side wall.
- There should be lots of space under the arm, with the elbow away from the body.
- The preparation is not as high as with the drive.
- A gentle pick-up of the racket head, which should be in rhythm with the pace of the ball.

Things Not to Do
- Do not raise the racket too high unless the ball is sitting up.
- Do not cock the wrist nor have the elbow too tight to the body.
- Do not grip the racket too tightly.
- Do not have an excessive swing.

Fig 71 Approach on forehand lob is lower than the drive.

Fig 72 (LEFT)
Racket head is open
to lift ball high on
front wall.

Fig 73 (BELOW)
Extend shoulder
and wrist on
follow-through.

Delivery

Points to Remember
- The racket head is laid back into the flat-bottom swing, coming into the ball with the leading edge.
- The racket and arm are out in front of the opponent.
- Release the elbow and wrist with extension of the forearm.
- The racket head should be open.
- Take the racket head to the floor directly under the ball with an open racket face.
- At impact, the racket face should be thrown directly to the ceiling; this takes the ball high on to the front wall.
- Strike the ball in front of your leading leg.

Things Not to Do
- Do not have a closed face at impact.
- Do not jab at the ball; feel the ball on to the strings.

- Do not hit the ball too hard.
- Do not hold the grip with too much tension.

Follow-Through

Points to Remember
- A gentle follow-through with an extension of the shoulder to direct and feel the ball.
- Carry the follow-through up to the ceiling to trace the path of the ball into the back corner, which will help you recover to the 'T'.

Things Not to Do
- Do not be too quick with the follow-through.
- Do not quit on the follow-through.
- Do not keep the elbow bent.

Fig 74 Watching the ball flight on follow-through.

THE BACKHAND LOB

Preparation

Follow the guidance given for the forehand drive. On the backhand you should hit the ball off the right leg.

Points to Remember
- Correct grip.
- A slight movement of the racket head away from the body towards the side wall.
- There should be plenty of space under the arm, with the elbow away from the body.
- The preparation is not as high as with the drive.
- A gentle pick-up of the racket head which should be in rhythm with the pace of the ball.

Things Not to Do
- Do not raise the racket too high unless the ball is sitting up.
- Do not cock the wrist nor have the elbow too tight to the body.
- Do not grip the racket too tightly.
- Do not have an excessive swing.

Delivery

Points to Remember
- The racket head is laid back into the flat-bottom swing, coming into the ball with the leading edge.
- The racket and arm are out in front of the opponent.
- Release the elbow and wrist with extension of the forearm.
- The racket head should be open.
- Take the racket head to the floor directly under the ball with an open racket face.
- At impact, the racket face should be thrown directly to the ceiling; this takes the ball high on to the front wall.

Fig 75 Approach on backhand lob is lower than the drive.

Fig 76 Racket head is open to lift ball high on front wall.

Fig 77 Follow through towards ceiling.

Fig 78 Recoil to rest at 'T'.

- Strike the ball in front of your leading leg.
- This technique is used for both straight and cross-court lobs.

Things Not to Do
- Do not have a closed face at impact.
- Do not jab at the ball, feel the ball on to the strings.
- Do not hit the ball too hard.
- Do not hold the grip with too much tension.

Follow-Through

Points to Remember
- A gentle follow-through with an extension of the shoulder to direct and feel the ball.
- Carry the follow-through up to the ceiling to trace the path of the ball into the

back corner, which will help you to recover to the 'T'.

Things Not to Do
- Do not be too quick with the follow-through.
- Do not quit on the follow-through.
- Do not keep the elbow bent.

BASIC SERVING TECHNIQUES

The Lob Serve

This is the most effective service method. Obviously one foot must be in the service-box area.

Hold the ball in your non-playing hand. The technique used is the same as the lob.

Points to Remember

- Always look at your opponent before serving.
- Look to hit the ball high on the front wall.
- Aim just over halfway across the front wall.
- Make sure the ball is dropping steeply into the opposite back corner, hitting the side wall.
- Make sure as you serve that you move direct to the 'T'.

The Flat Serve

Players use this serve most commonly. With one foot in the service-box area and holding the ball in your non-playing hand, the technique used is the same as the volley.

Points to Remember

- Always look at your opponent before serving.
- Look to hit the ball just above the cut line on the front wall.

Fig 79 (ABOVE) Open face for lob serve.
Fig 80 (BELOW) Always look at your opponent on flat serve.

Fig 81 Racket is up and ready for receiving serve.

- The ball should come at your opponent at a sharp angle off the side wall, at the back of the service box.
- Make sure as you serve that you move direct to the 'T'.
- You must hit the side wall (stopping your opponent from volleying).

- You must move to the 'T' as you serve (so your opponent cannot catch you out of position).
- You must be aware of your opponent (do not watch the front wall).

Return of Serve

The return of serve is vital to construct a good rally. Many people do not return well, immediately placing themselves under pressure; this causes the rally to break down early. If you can return well you will find that once you are into a rally it will last longer.

Points to Remember
- Stand at the corner of the service box away from the sidewall.
- Hold the racket up at volleying height.
- Your chest should be facing the side wall to receive the serve.
- Make sure you are looking at your opponent when he is serving (do not stare at the front wall).
- When your opponent serves always look to volley the ball, with the volley technique and aim to hit it high on the front wall straight into the back corner; this will give you time to move into the 'T' position.
- You must not let the ball drop into the back corner.
- You must not frequently hit cross-court (if you do, ensure that there is good width).
- You must not hit to the front too often; this increases the likelihood of errors.

CHAPTER 4

The Practice Game

Was it Gary Player who said, 'The more I practise, the luckier I get', or was it Jahangir Khan? Did you ever watch Player's perfect putting? Or were you ever treated to one of those extraordinary Jahangir warm-up routines when he would start volleying the ball close to the forehand front wall, retreat down the court, still volleying until he was against the back wall, advance again to the service line, play a quick figure of eight on the volley and then repeat the whole trick on the backhand wall? It was often better than anything to be seen in the subsequent match, and more times than not it rattled his opponent.

Practice is the bedrock of all physical activity. Driving a car, riding a bicycle, hitting a ball – all the things we do without conscious thought are actually the product of ingrained practice and squash is no exception. In fact, so perverse and contrary are many of the things we do in producing rebound effects on a squash court that practice becomes paramount. We have to be able to reach into our mental and physical skills locker at a split second's notice and find the precise shot, the precise weight and the precise angle to deal with every arising situation, while at the same time thinking about our opponent's ability to change that situation with his own skills and deception. Practice is the engraving of the game into your unconscious memory bank.

Ideally, a committed player should practise for 30 or 40min every day. Of course, no one

except a professional can find the time, or perhaps even the motivation, to practise with such regular intensity. But if you are going to succeed in this game at any level, you should be prepared to commit to at least two practice sessions a week, in addition to any other training and competition you may undertake.

Many players waste their practice sessions on the meaningless repetition of their strongest or most enjoyable strokes and ploys. In fact, practice should be as much about addressing weaknesses as honing strengths.

You should go into every practice session with specific aims and targets. Today video analysis may show you the areas that need attention more readily than any criticism from coaches or your own in-match analysis. You might decide to spend a session striving for full arm extension in the drive, correct foot approach to the backhand boast or proper recoil recovery to the 'T' from a volley drop. You may work on a better lob service, a cross-court return nick shot or a high overhead cut into the top corners of the court.

Solo practice should be a fairly intense affair. Find a quiet court away from any audience. Try to analyse what you are doing well or badly and try to improve on it. Do not simply knock a ball about. Select a shot or a movement to work on, perhaps mix it up with another complementary action, and give yourself a set number of repetitions in each burst of activity. While working, concentrate on studying your own actions, the degree of accuracy achieved and in what ways you are failing to make the shot or the movement perfect. You might need the eye and the advice of a coach or a practice partner to spot the faults and improvements. A camcorder on one practice session can sometimes be more instructive than a dozen competitive matches.

The practice court should be a silent, almost monastic place. The headphones favoured by many younger professionals are mostly for visual impact upon any watching admirers. You may be able to relax to your favourite tracks, but you cannot concentrate properly on what you are doing. There is an intellectual content in practice that allows for reflection upon what you can do, what you are doing and what you should be doing. You cannot do that to music.

If you have not practised before or not for some time, twenty repetitions at a time will probably be comfortable. But fifty at a time should be the normal activity rate you strive for.

It often helps to find a practice partner with whom you can study both your own and his progress and come to understand the progress you have both made. Pairs practice extends the range of activity and the pace of preparation, allowing each of you to seek the level of unconscious capability required in playing circumstances, approaching the speed and demand of actual competition.

Relief from routine and an expansion of social enjoyment in practice can be achieved in pairs games, triples play or two-against-one games in which scoring may be introduced and the pressure varied by rotating the heavier demand of the rallies.

It is important, though, that all practice is structured to the aim of improvement rather than just activity. Coaches sometimes confuse quantity with quality. Four hours of endless routines can only lead to disillusionment. An hour or so of carefully structured stroke and rally practice can leave you thirsting to put it all to the test in the next competitive match.

There follows a range of practice formats for the strokes we discuss in this book, all of which should be played with close attention to the correct stroke play described earlier. There are other practice routines – every coach has his own favourites – and you may have your own ways of practising with which you are comfortable.

THE STRAIGHT DRIVE

Solo Practice

Bounce the ball on the wall behind the backhand 'T' and boast backhand to the top forehand corner leading on the front foot, then come round on the ball to step into the forehand drive on the correct foot to drive the ball straight to make it fade in the back corner. Then bounce the ball on the wall behind the forehand 'T' and boast forehand to the top backhand corner leading on the front foot, then come round on the ball to step into the backhand drive on the correct foot to drive the ball straight to make the ball fade in the back corner.

Pairs Practice

With both players working from the 'T', the deep player boasts from the deep backhand corner using the correct footwork and returns to the 'T'; the front court player drives straight, using the correct technique, ensuring that the ball fades in the back corner and returns to the 'T'; the deep player then boasts from the deep forehand corner, using the correct footwork and returns to the 'T'; the front court player then drives straight, using the correct technique, ensuring that the ball fades in the back corner and returns to the 'T'.

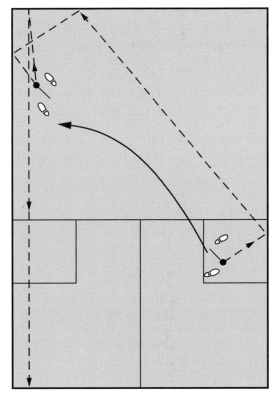

Fig 82

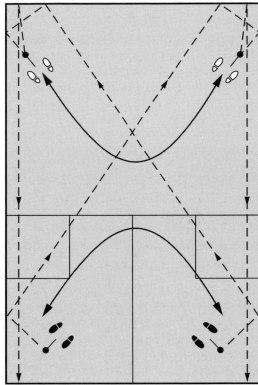

Fig 83

This same boast-and-drive routine may be varied for backhand drives and cross-court drives on either hand. Towards the end of a practice session, it is useful to perform at least one repeated session with the front court player mixing the forehand, backhand and cross-court drives, while the deep player reacts with the required boast – always using the correct technique, adopting the correct footwork and returning to the 'T' between shots.

THE CROSS-COURT DRIVE

Solo Practice

Bounce the ball on the wall behind the backhand 'T' and boast backhand to the top forehand corner, leading on the front foot; come round on the ball to step into the forehand drive on the correct feet to drive the ball cross-court to make the ball fade in the back corner. Then bounce the ball on the wall behind the forehand 'T' and boast forehand to the top backhand corner, leading on the front foot, come round on the ball to step into the backhand drive on the correct feet to drive the ball cross-court to make the ball fade in the back corner.

Pairs Practice

With both players working from the 'T', the deep player boasts from the deep backhand corner, using the correct footwork and returns to the 'T'; the front court player drives cross-court, using the correct technique and ensuring that the ball fades in the back corner and returns to the 'T'. After twenty repetitions the front court player hits one straight drive on the forehand to bring the deep player across to the forehand and the practice switches to the backhand cross-court drive for another twenty repetitions.

The advice we gave at the end of the section on the straight drive applies equally well here too.

THE VOLLEY

Solo Practice

Stand a yard or so from the front wall on either forehand or backhand, bounce the ball and tap it up to create the first volley close to the side wall, then make twenty volleyed repetitions. Do the same from mid court and again from just behind the service box.

When this has been mastered, you could aim to develop the practice to the point where you can perform the repetitions without a break, aiming for the favoured warm-up of the legendary Jahangir Khan which we described at the beginning of this chapter, remembering also his quick figure-of-eight series to change hands. The figure-of-eight itself provides useful volley practice both high and low. Standing in mid court at the appropriate distance from the front wall, throw the ball to the front wall to create the first volley, strike, then volley first on one hand and then the other to the front corner

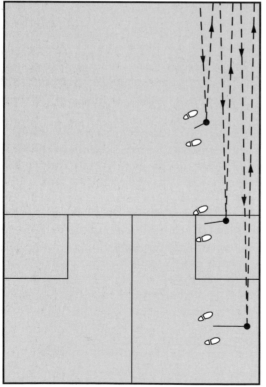

Fig 84

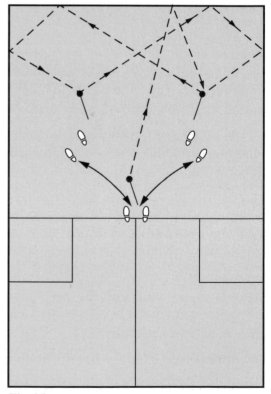

Fig 85

so that the rebound from the side wall flies to the racket face on the opposing hand, repeat twenty times. It may be easier to start this figure-of-eight exercise on the half-volley until the footwork and opposing racket swings are mastered.

Pairs Practice

Working from the 'T', one player feeds the ball to the required length on the volley and the other comes from the 'T' to volley straight and then goes to ghost a shot on the other side of the court as the first player picks up the ball and delivers it for the same length on that side and another straight volley begins the sequence again for from twenty to fifty repetitions.

The same sequence may be created for the cross-court volley, and the feeder can be challenged himself if the volleying player mixes up straight and cross-court volleys from the chosen length. Between every shot both players should seek to return to the 'T'.

THE LOB

Solo Practice

Throw the ball to the front wall so that it drops close to the front corner on either hand, then step in from the 'T' to lift the ball, as described earlier, either straight down the wall or cross-court, making sure that the length is sufficient to take your opponent to the back corner but not enough to allow him

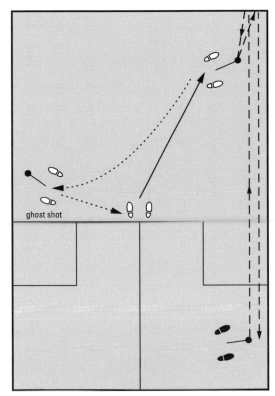

Fig 86

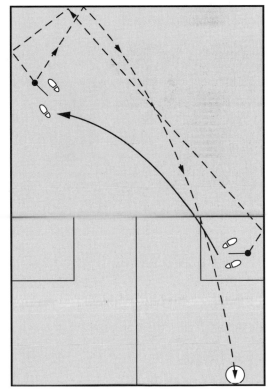

Fig 87

the convenience of waiting for a long rebound from the back wall, then recoil to the 'T'.

A continuous routine can be developed by lobbing cross-court, recoiling through the 'T' to retrieve the deep ball with a straight drive, then boasting this and moving up through the 'T' to hit a straight lob, recoiling again through the 'T' to retrieve the ball with a straight drive, then boasting to set the routine up again.

Pairs Practice

Boast and lob varying from straight to cross-court, with the front court player recoiling to the 'T' between each shot and the deep player changing sides via the 'T' is as simple, and exhausting, an exercise as the practice court can offer, yet a deeply satisfying one if a sustained rhythm is established; it is easily played as a point-scoring competition.

THE DROP SHOT

Solo Practice

On either hand bounce the ball deep in the court, boast it to the opposing top corner and move through the 'T' to drop either straight or cross-court, making sure to recoil to the 'T'.

Pairs Practice

One player bounces the ball and delivers it to the chosen length and the other player

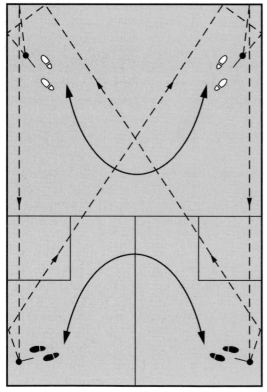

Fig 88

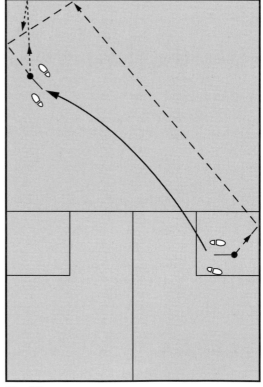

Fig 89

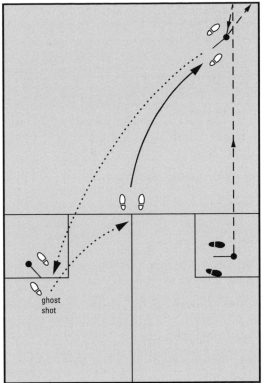

Fig 90

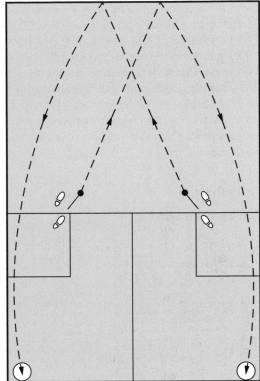

Fig 91

moves from the 'T' to play a drop shot, either straight or cross-court, on the full or the half volley, then recoils to the 'T', plays a ghost boast and then returns to the 'T', while the first player collects the ball and delivers another play-pace feed for a drop from the chosen length.

Long drop practice for one player may also become lob practice for the other, switching the lob from straight to cross-court each time to keep the practice rally going. The deep player can either drop straight or cut across the court.

THE SERVICE

The service is the only free shot in the game. It is amazing how often players just push the ball into play without any apparent fore-thought when regular practice can make it into a point-scorer. A few repetitions on your own each day can lead to your knowing all the variations of the service, but remember to practise with a ball similarly warm to the one you would be playing with in a match.

With a bucket placed on the spot where the ideal lob service should hit the floor, it is possible to establish for yourself where the service should hit the front wall, deflect off the side wall and brush against the back wall to create the maximal discomfort for your opponent. Ideally the ball should float around the outside edges of the receiving box, dropping to the side wall just below the top court line and to the back wall gently enough to strike the floor just a few inches into the back court.

The flat service should ideally fly either to the side-wall nick or the back-wall nick. You will notice that many players serve backhand from the forehand side. This is to narrow the angle of rebound from the side wall and thus keep the ball as far from the receiver's racket as possible throughout the serve. Only through practice can you establish whether this suits your style and angle of delivery, or if you could be more testing to your opponent by delivering a wide angle by serving from close to the wall on either side.

MOVEMENT

Ghosting is the easiest of practices for pure movement. Classic rallies can be played without the inconvenience of an opponent in order to perfect the footwork and balance the changes required to move correctly from one shot to another by way of the 'T'.

The variations will come to you easily enough for ghosting, if only actual rallies could be so easily controlled, and it should be a mandatory part of every practice session. If you can educate your body to the demands of pure movement on the court it will leave your mind free for more important tactical and competitive matters in real play.

With a ball, you can keep drop and volley routines going endlessly while concentrating on the footwork and body shifts that will carry you from one shot to the other by way of the 'T'. The figure-of-eight played at a low level and on the half-volley is also a splendid exercise with which to perfect front court movement. A slight angle on mid-court drives will provide the exercise from which to learn lunging from the 'T' and recoiling back to it, especially with a partner delivering the drive for you from your front court pick-ups.

CONDITIONED GAMES

Practice can be fun as well as gruellingly intense. There are many conditioned games which can be designed to emphasize particular skills or movements in a structure that allows the participants to win or lose, using American point-per-rally scoring to 15 points over one, three or five games.

Straight against All-Action

One player is allowed to play a normal all-court game, but the other can hit the ball only straight – to any length, but always straight. Best of one, three or five with an alternate restriction to straight play until and unless a deciding game is required in which both players revert to all-court action.

Full-Court Driving

Both players have to hit every ball to bounce behind the half-court line. Normal American scoring and rules apply, but the rally is lost if a ball bounces in front of the half-court line. Best of one, three or five with an all-court decider if necessary.

Alley Play

A normal game but the ball has to bounce within the width of the service box on either hand. Any ball that bounces in the centre of the court is out and the rally is lost. Best of one, three or five with an all-court decider if required.

Variable Scoring

If you are practising with a player of a higher or lower standard than yourself you can play a normal match of one, three or five games with one player (the better one) scoring traditionally hand-in and hand-out while the other (the less good one) scores a point per rally.

Front and Back

One player takes the front court from which he can hit only to the deep court behind the half-court line; the other takes the deep court from which he can hit only short to the front court. Normal play otherwise; you can change roles at whatever frequency suits your requirements. Best of one, three or five with a normal all-court decider if required.

Triples

One player takes the forehand side, another the backhand side and the third plays an all-court normal game. The all-court player scores until he loses a rally, then the forehand player takes the all-court scoring role, the backhand player becomes the forehand player and the all-court player becomes the back-hand player, and so on. Best of one, three or five – or until someone falls over; this can be extremely testing.

CHAPTER 5

The Tactical Game

There are people who go on to a squash court without a single thought about what they intend to do; they may just do a few stretches, pick up the racket, warm up the ball and start playing. Sometimes they play astonishingly well. Sometimes they win. More often they lose.

Just as it is important that the body be warmed and prepared for the task ahead, so should the mind. This is not a leisure pursuit, not a fun game in which everybody has a good time. This is battle to the death: physical chess, boxing without brain damage. Squash is a hard, physical game, but it is a thinking game also. Winning at squash means driving the opponent to defeat. You might gain a few points from brilliance. You might take a game on pure athletic superiority. You will only win matches by being tactically astute before, during and after the action.

GAME PLAN

Before you start your match you should have a clear plan on how you are going to play tactically. The first aspect is what are you trying to achieve: do not just turn up and play with no preparation, dashing from the office straight on to the court with no clear tactical plan. If you are playing a league match try to arrive 20min to half an hour before your match. Once changed, start your warm-up; during this period you should be going over your game plan in your head. If you are playing an opponent you have seen or played before you should have a good idea of his (or her) strengths and weaknesses. The privacy of your own warm-up is a good time to start building a mental picture. If you have not met before, you will want to use the knock-up as much for assessing his strengths and weaknesses as for readying you own game.

OPPONENT ANALYSIS

The battle starts from a tactical viewpoint not at the end of the knock-up but from the beginning of your first conversation with your opponent. He will send you information from the very first word. Of course, your opponent may have read this chapter too. He might be sending misinformation also and so you have to be alert for a perceptive analysis.

Beware of the 'mummy', the over-bandaged player who may have nothing wrong with him at all but be using a preliminary tactic to reduce your aggression and even raise a little sympathy on your part. He will probably be moving like a greyhound by the time you are approaching the end of the first game.

If you have met before, try to assess how he feels about the last outcome. If not, what does he know, or think he knows, about you

Fig 92 The dressing room encounter: part of the match

and your game? This should help you to prise out valuable nuggets of experience gained from the last encounter.

Talk about the day: if he has had a bad day at work you know that you should start well by taking him while he is still off balance. If it was a long day for him you might think about extending the early part of the match to take some of his remaining energy away.

Perhaps he will refer to an injury that would cause you to move him about rather sharply during the match to exploit any actual or feared residual damage.

He might mention the last player he encountered and what happened. If you have played the same person, you might gain some idea of how to deal with this new opponent's best approaches.

If you are treated to a diatribe of victories and apparently boundless confidence, you may well be witnessing insecurity in action, or at least picking up a few tips on how not to play against him.

Watch your opponent's preparation during the pre-match period and his conversation. If there has been more chat than warm-up, you will know that the early points of the match will need to be fast and fierce to exploit his unready state.

If the dressing room encounter reveals a quiet, non-communicative character who warms up properly and provides you with almost no information about anything, get ready for a tough match. But make sure that you have a good chat over a drink after the action; you might learn much that could be useful when you meet him again.

WARM-UP AND WARM-DOWN

The warm-up is an essential part of preparation for your match. The warm-up mobilizes the athlete mentally and physically. This will improve performance and reduce the possibility of injury. The warm-up will increase your body temperature and your heart rate. Circulation and muscle metabolism will increase. How to achieve this is through aerobic activity, stretching and resistance exercises. In squash try to use stretching or aerobic exercises that are specific to the sport. The intensity should be enough to produce mild sweat without fatigue.

After play it is equally essential that you warm down, which should happen immediately after your match. The reason for this is that it reduces post-exercise sourness and allows for a controlled reduction of your heart rate and respiration. The warm-down should include stretching similar to that in the warm-up as this reduces the possibility of muscle injury. Stretching in the warm-up and the warm-down should be slow and sustained for a 15 to 30sec hold and repeated up to five times. Remember to give yourself 20min to warm up and again to cool down. This will help you to recover soon enough to be able to have a match the following day.

THE PRE-MATCH KNOCK-UP

The knock-up (say for 5min) is not just to get the ball warm and ready for play, it is rather a time in which to analyse your opponent's strengths and weaknesses. The questions to ask and the areas to look at are:

- Does he have the correct grip?
- Is his technique up to standard?

Fig 93 The drink at the bar: part of the next match.

- Can he retrieve the ball out of the back two corners?
- Does he have problems taking a ball that is tight to the wall?
- Use the lob to see how he copes with the volley.
- Does your opponent bend or not?
- Does he like to volley or not?
- Put the ball to the front of the court to see whether he wants to move quickly forward or not.
- Make sure the ball you are using is in good condition and suitable to your level of play.
- Remember that one side, either forehand or backhand, will generally be the weaker one for your opponent; you will want to know where to concentrate your attack, especially when you prise open the spaces into which the attack is to be concentrated.

Courts have their own characteristics. During the knock-up you should be considering the following:

- Is the front wall fast or slow?
- How high is the ceiling for the use of the lob?
- Is the floor sanded or sealed?
- Are any of the floorboards loose?
- How big is the nick?
- Is the court hot or cold?
- How bright are lights and do they flicker?
- Remember that the condition of the court will affect how you well you can implement your match tactics.

THE EARLY EXCHANGES

The early exchanges are of vital importance, they set the pattern of the match and a good start could well determine the outcome. Consider the following:

- Make sure that you have an increased heart rate at love all; do not let yourself warm-down in the knock-up.
- Make sure that the rallies are long and hard with no unforced errors.
- Most balls should be hit into the back corners.
- Dominate the 'T' to take the sting out of your opponent.
- Volley as much as possible to cut down your opponent's recovery time and to maintain pressure.
- Body language should be positive and dynamic, as if to dominate and to persuade your opponent that things can only get worse for him.
- Do not go short into the front two corners early; such obvious eagerness may appear to show nervousness; let your opponent understand that he is likely to be working this hard for the next two hours if necessary.
- Remember that early dominance often dictates the outcome of the match.

By now you should have refined your game plan to the point of implementation, although you will almost certainly need to adjust it as the match develops. Here are some points which amount to a universal game plan around which your actual tactics on the day will have been refined by the points noted above:

- Make sure that you warm up sufficiently and that your heart rate is increased before you start the knock-up.
- Make sure that you understand as much as possible at this stage about your opponent's strengths and weaknesses.
- Check the climate of your court: if it is hot make sure that you prepare for long rallies with the ball being returned regularly; if it is cold remind yourself to stand

high on the 'T' area because the ball will die quickly in the corners and the rallies will be short so be alert to cover your shots.

- Go on court determined to hit the four corners of the court consistently.
- You will want to dominate the 'T' area and to keep your opponent deep in the back corners away from it.
- Be aware that each opponent is different, even from the last time you met; do not use the same game plan every time you step on court.
- Store information on your opponents by reviewing every match in your head afterwards.

What not to do – and what to do – in your game plan:

- Do not hit cross-courts unless in conclusion of a rally designed to be finished in that way.
- Do not hit the boast too often; remember that the boast is an attacking shot and not always defensive.
- Do not just hit the ball hard all the time, vary the pace and, when you decide to hit hard, hit accurately.
- Do not hit the ball half court: short, easily intercepted drives will undermine any game plan. Go on court determined to hit a good length and good width whatever the situation.

SHOT SELECTION AND RALLY CONSTRUCTION

Shot selection is of vital importance. Every shot in the game has a purpose, from the basic drives to the nick shots. Below are the tactical reasons why each shot is played and how it is used.

The Forehand and Backhand Straight Drive

The basic drives are the most used and thus the most important shots in the game. They are used from every part of the court to put pressure on your opponent. The drive to the back of the court is described in Chapter 3. The tactical use of the drive can only happen if the technical aspects are applied correctly. You must hit the ball at the right height on the front wall so that it will fade away from the 'T' area where your opponent should be; as the ball reaches the back of the service box it will dip and die into the back corners (the ball must not bounce off more than 1ft from the back wall). If this approach is used the drive will put pressure on your opponent to move him from the 'T' as far into the back corners as possible. This tactic makes his recovery time out of the back corners to the 'T' more difficult, which will give you more time to use your game plan from the 'T' position. The front-court kill is played when you are in front of your opponent or when he is out of position away from the 'T' area. Front-court drives should be used sparingly and not so as to appear ostentatious. All drives are used to vary the pace of the game; they are not just hit hard and low and the entire front wall is to be used. Remember that the basic drives are your 'bread-and-butter' shots.

The Cross-Court Drive

Cross-court drives are to be used either to move your opponent off the 'T' or to kill the ball. When aiming for the former all cross-courts must be hit wide and into the opposite side wall at differing heights on the front wall, with variation of pace and not just hard and low. The cross-court kill is used when your opponent is out of position and not on the

'T'. Remember that this drive should have the same fading and dying effect into the back two corners. It can be one of the best shots in the game, or one of the worst if it is not executed correctly (refer to the technical chapter). You must not hit the cross-court drive through the middle of the court as your opponent will cut the ball off at the 'T' area, making you work into one of the four corners and preventing you from dominating the 'T'.

The Volley

The volley is the second most important shot in the game. The volley, if played well, cuts your opponent's time down so that he is constantly under pressure. The volley enables you to dominate the 'T' area and to keep the middle of the court so that you are in a good position when opportunities arise. Do not always try to hit the ball hard on the volley. You can use it to apply pressure by chipping the ball higher on the front wall into the back two corners.

The Forehand and Backhand Drop and the Volley Drop

The drop and the volley drop shots are used to move your opponent to the front of the court when he is behind you and you are around the 'T'. When playing the drop make sure that the ball has hit the front wall about 2 or 3in above the tin, with the fading action causing it to dip tight to the side wall. As you will have the 'T' area when the ball is returned, if it is not a good return you will be able to attack and make your opponent move to one of the back two corners. The drop and the volley drop are normally used when your drives or volleys have been hit deep into the back to corners forcing your opponent away from the 'T' area. This will

give you an opportunity to play the drops and the volley drops with plenty of time, not resulting in an error because you feel that your opponent is close to you on the 'T' area. Remember that drops and volley drops are used to move your opponent and not to look for a winner to finish the rally; you have already set the trap for the winner of pressure on the return.

The Boast

The boast, like the drop and the volley drop, is a moving shot and not always defensive. The boast is most commonly used behind each service box to move your opponent quickly into the front corners by using the same tactical principals as with the drop and the volley drop. Always cover the boast by moving on to the 'T' area to cover a weak return as your opponent is out of position. If the return is good you have at least moved your opponent physically off the 'T'. Over time this will eventually tire him out as he is having to cover the four corners of the court. The boast may also be used when you are in front of your opponent on the 'T' by using an attacking or volley boast once again to move your opponent quickly.

The Lob

The lob, if played well, is a reliever of pressure. It gives you time to recover to the 'T' as your opponent cannot attack the ball on the volley. Use the lob when you are stretching or want time to relax and slow the game down. The lob, again if played correctly (*see* Chapter 3), puts direct pressure back on your opponent after you have been in a defensive position, which will frustrate him.

Remember that when the ball is tight (when it is close to the wall or below the height of the tin or you are under pressure) give it height.

Progressive analysis of your opponent's performance should lead to adaptations in your own tactics. Your plan before you play is generally set, since with luck you will have seen your opponent play. But what might occur is that he will also have seen you play and will have his own game plan organized. As the match progresses you should be able to arrive at a continuous analysis of his tactics and your own. A few examples of this might be the following.

- Your opponent thinks that you have a weak backhand so he keeps putting the ball in that area which causes you to make errors. Your reaction should be to put the ball in an area where your opponent is limited on where he can put the ball on your backhand.
- As the match progresses you might find that your opponent is tiring quicker than expected; if this is the case, use the drop, the boast or the volley. Take the ball earlier to put pressure on him. This will cause him to move constantly under pressure.
- In your own game you might find that your favourite shot is not working; take note of this and adjust accordingly by excluding it from your game for a period in the match. This might happen through loss of confidence or nervousness. Be patient, since you will usually find that the shot will return as you get into the rhythm of the match.

Remember always to have a pre-match game plan, but be ready for changes to take place, either from your opponent's play or yours in the way that you are playing. A key period for the reassessment of a game plan is between games when you have 90sec in which to re-evaluate.

POST-MATCH ANALYSIS

After your match, whether you have won or lost, never just dash into the shower, always give yourself time to assess the outcome; a good time for this is during the warm-down. Most players will put a loss down to simply playing badly and will not want to think about the match because their pride is hurt.

Post-match analysis is essential to your learning of the game tactically: if you learn from this assessment, during the next time you compete the same mistakes are unlikely to occur as often. You can also ask people who watched your game for an unbiased opinion or, even better, ask a coach. Sometimes, instead of having a lesson with a professional, pay him to watch you in competition and then to advise you on your future tactics.

This chapter has dealt with fundamental tactics applied through the basic drives and on through every sensible shot in the game. Tactics should be used in a simple way. Do not over-complicate this aspect by being too clever in what you are trying to achieve. Here is the essence of what simple tactics should be aiming for:

- Getting higher on the 'T' than your opponent does.
- Dominating the 'T'.
- Taking the ball as early as possible.
- Placing the ball into the gaps created by your rallying away from your opponent.
- Playing dying shots that will not rebound out of the corners.

If you can make all your on-court effort work direct towards this tactical framework, you will in time be able to cope with the more advanced situations in match play more readily and naturally.

CHAPTER 6

The Picture Game

Analysis of a player's performance is an integral aspect of good coaching. Analysis plays a part in so many things you do: the analysis of technique; the analysis of teaching methods; the selection and use of equipment; the examination of injuries; and tactical analysis. All coaches use analysis, whether they are conscious of it or not, and every player uses some sort of analysis, although not always too well, in reaching for improvement.

Every time you talk about new tactics or attempt post-performance feedback, some

Fig 94 Stafford Murray at the camcorder.

form of analysis is taking place. The experienced and successful coach quite rightly sets great store about his interpretation of performance; the point about analysis is that you can use it to enhance your own subjective appraisal and improve both your own effectiveness and your players' performance.[1]

Feedback about performance is an important part of coaching and self-improvement. In order to provide feedback we need to analyse what is actually happening on court. Most experienced coaches will be good analysts in that the feedback they give to their players is objective and does not contain too much personal bias. But until a coach can actually show a player what he is doing on court or the player can record his play for his own later inspection, it is often difficult to arrive at a solution for repetitive errors or hidden weaknesses.

It is impossible for anyone to recall all the events that take place in a squash match. If you assume that there are a thousand shots in a match, there will be at least a thousand pieces of information that a coach is trying objectively to make judgements on. Research has shown that even the best coaches in the world can recall only around 30 per cent of the information that they observe in a match; therefore 70 per cent of it has been lost. So why do humans struggle to recall all this information? From scientific observation, performance tends to suffer from five rudimentary weaknesses:

- Memory overload: too many bits of information to remember;
- Subjective bias: personal feelings can hide the truth;
- Halo effect: coaches will naturally have favourite players;
- Leniency error: the tendency to remember either the best or the worst events; and
- Highlighting: remembering extraordinary shots but not bread-and-butter work.

In order to give fair and objective feedback to players, these problem areas need to be minimized. We have found an ideal method to be a combination of video and notational analysis. By taping the match or coaching practice we have a record of this performance that we can systematically go through afterwards and where we can objectively analyse the areas we are interested in. Both of these methods have also been proved to work as strong motivational tools.

VIDEO ANALYSIS

The video camera can be used as a tool to enhance learning and further our understanding in squash. We have found that its use with players offers the following bonuses:

- The 'Bucks Fizz' theory: the camera never lies, therefore performers will not be able to doubt your analysis;
- The 'serial criminal' theory: you now have a permanent record; it is now possible to review the event and produce a more accurate analysis;
- The 'Andy Grey' theory: you can now analyse aspects that you are not normally able to;
- The 'hand-break' theory: you now have the ability to stop the tape at any given point for detailed analysis and/or feedback; and

- The 'Mr Motivator' theory: it has been proved that by watching successful performances players can become naturally more focused and motivated.

It is clear that video can be used as an ideal tool for the provision of feedback. The images produced can act as a strong motivational influence, enhance analysis procedures and assist in adherence to technical decisions and continuity in practice and play.

By watching video images of themselves, players are able to assess subjectively the strengths and weaknesses in their games and then compare these findings with the thoughts of the coach. Again this acts as a good evaluation technique, raising the technical and tactical awareness of the player. It also provides an excellent opportunity for the player to compare his shot selection, movement and technique with that of any chosen role model.

There are, however, several points that need to be established before the video is used by coach and player. The coach needs the trust of the player that can only grow from a sound working relationship. Secondly, the coach needs to ensure that, if the manipulation of events occurs, it must advantageous to the player and not a particular view being pressed by the coach. Finally, the exercise must be adopted as a mutual endeavour in which the coach is often learning as much from the player as the player is learning from the coach.

NOTATIONAL ANALYSIS

According to Hughes,[2] notational analysis is an objective way of recording performance so that the key elements of it can be quantified in a valid and consistent manner. In other words, to find out what really happened as opposed to what you think may have happened. Notational analysis will be employed in two main areas: technical and tactical analysis.

Technical Analysis

In squash a good technique leads to efficiency of movement. Inefficient movement wastes energy and success demands that energy is expended in the most efficient way possible.[3] When looking at technical analysis we need to know what an 'ideal' performance looks like so that we can compare our performance to this one. When we have this ideal data image then comparisons can be made to highlight major or minor discrepancies and weaknesses.

Tactical Analysis

Strategy and tactics are two vital features of squash, so sound tactical analysis is vital. There are many areas that need attention when analysing tactics such as winner and error ratios, short and long shots, volley distributions and shot selection from specific corners. These can be simply analysed by using pen and paper and devising your own system. The book *Notational Analysis of Sport* by Mike Hughes and Ian Franks is the authority when it comes to information on hand-notation systems.

Simple data, such as the distribution of winners and errors, may be done during a match. However, when the analysis becomes more complex (such as the distribution of all volleys) the camcorder stores the information for more detailed notation. It will become clear as time goes on where points are being won and lost, where rallies can be shortened or lengthened, why vital points are being sacrificed by habitual blocking, and so on. It will eventually all be there on the paper for coach and player to inspect. So pick up your pen and paper, grab the camcorder and start designing the framework in which your racket can become more effective.

Notes

1. Sharpe, B., *Analysis of Performance* (National Coaching Foundation, Springfield Books, 1989).
2. Hughes, M.D., 'Computerised Notation of Racket Sports', in T. Rielly, M.D. Hughes and A. Lees (eds), *Science and Racket Sports* (London: E. & F. Spon, 1995, pp. 249–56).
3. Franks, I.M. and G. Millar, 'Eye Witness Testimony in Sport', *Journal of Sport Behaviour*, vol. 9 (1984, pp. 38–45).

CHAPTER 7

The Body Game

The game of squash presents significant physical challenges at any level. In order to plan an effective physical training programme for it we first need to understand exactly what we are preparing the body for. Most of our work is with elite players whose performance levels require intense training. Obviously a part-time, league ten club player is not going to have the time, inclination or demand for the sort of preparation work normal for a world-ranked professional.

But it is a matter of degree. The demands on the lower-level player are no less stressful than those on the professional. Indeed, it could be argued that the relatively weaker, slower, less flexible club player may be under more stress in trying to climb up from the bottom of the game. The first absolutely basic requirement for any player who wants to do more than run around flailing at the ball is to understand the physical requirements of the game itself.

TIME ANALYSIS

At elite level, matches usually last anywhere from 45min up to 2hr or more in extreme circumstances. At club level it is more common for matches to last between 25 and 45min. The only formal rest allowed in between games is 90sec (or 2min for professional men) and breaks between rallies are typically approximately 7 to 10sec in length. Rallies may last from only a few seconds up to 30sec or more. In the elite men's game the average rally length is approximately 20sec or twelve shots, and in the elite women's game it is 12sec or eight shots. Although not very common, rallies of nearly 3min have been recorded in recent elite men's competitions.

PHYSIOLOGICAL ANALYSIS

One of the easiest ways to assess the physical demands of a sport is to monitor a performer's heart rate during the event. In squash we have measured players of all standards and found that the heart-rate response is similar across all ability levels. The rate rises during the first few minutes of play and then remains relatively stable at about 85–90 per cent of the maximum. For an individual with a maximum heart rate of 200 beats per minute, this would mean that his rate would remain in the region of 170 to 180 beats per minute for the duration of the match. It is important to remember that, although the heart-rate responses are similar across standards, this is relative to the fitness level of the performer. Due to his superior level of fitness, an elite player will be able to maintain a much higher intensity of play for a longer period of time than a club player will.

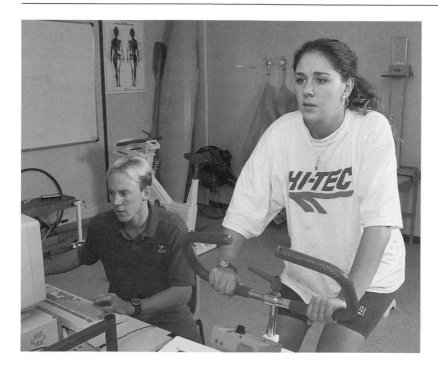

Fig 95 Cassie Campion works while Damon Brown records.

MOVEMENT ANALYSIS

Squash presents unique movement challenges to the performer. It is a sport that requires the development of speed over short distances. If a player is moving diagonally across the court from the back corner to the front corner, the furthest distance he is likely to cover in a straight line without changing direction is 8m. When a player is moving from the middle of the court ('T') to the ball the furthest movement into the back corners will normally be no more than 3.5m and 4.5m into the front corners. A player needs to have the ability to change direction smoothly at speed and will be required to perform a series of lunging, twisting and stretching actions to reach the ball and recover position. For the smooth execution of shots, a player needs to perform all movements in a position of balance and control. Squash is a sport requiring multidirectional movements performed over short distances with regular changes of direction and for sustained periods.

From the time and physiological analysis of the game it is clear that, to be successful, a player will need good levels of aerobic fitness and local muscular endurance to cope with repetitive movements to and from the ball and the duration and intensity of a match. However, a player also requires speed, strength, power, agility and flexibility to deal with the movement challenges imposed by the game. Squash is a weight-bearing sport so the appropriate bodily composition will also be important for success.

COMPONENTS OF FITNESS FOR SQUASH

Aerobic Fitness

Aerobic fitness or endurance refers to the capacity to continue prolonged physical activity and to delay the beginning of fatigue. In squash the ability to maintain a high pace of play for the duration of a match without the onset of significant fatigue is critical to success. If your aerobic fitness is low then you will find it difficult to recover between rallies and games and you will begin to get tired towards the later stages of a match. Aerobic fitness is important during training as it will help you get more from your workouts, particularly during interval training sessions, where aerobic fitness fosters the ability to recover quickly between successive exercise bouts.

Muscular Endurance

Virtually every time you play a shot during a match you will generally have to push away from the 'T', step in and out of your shot and push back towards the 'T'. These repeated actions place a lot of stress on the muscles in the legs and, without good muscular endurance, your legs will start to feel heavy and fatigue will set in rapidly. Once your legs begin to suffer fatigue your movement will become impaired, you will not be able to get to the ball so quickly and you will struggle to get into the right position to execute your shots. A player with good muscular endurance will be able to withstand the repetitive movements to and from the ball without becoming fatigued, giving him a significant advantage over an opponent with poor muscular endurance.

Speed

Speed derives from the ability to move the body quickly around the court. Speed in squash can be useful in attack, giving a player the ability to move on to the ball early and create pressure on the opponent. Speed is also essential in defence since it enables a player to pick up attacking shots, particularly in the front of the court. Leg speed is clearly required but arm speed is also necessary in helping to generate pace on the shot. In addition to speed of movement, speed of thought in reacting and anticipating are other important components.

Strength

Strength in the legs, abdomen and lower back are important in squash. Strength is used in helping to develop powerful movements away from the 'T', maintaining the stability of the body during shot execution and in holding a balanced position on the 'T'. Strong players are often referred to as having 'solid' movement. Strength helps a player to move in a controlled and efficient manner around the court and is important in enabling a player to control his bodyweight when moving quickly on to the ball. It is quite common to see players 'falling through the shot' if they do not have suitable levels of leg and torso strength.

Power

To be a powerful player you need to be able to develop force, that is, to apply strength at speed. Power helps a player to move explosively away from the 'T' and to recover quickly from a deep lunge position so that he can clear his shot and get back into position on the 'T'. Most movements on the court involve some contribution from power since there is a need to develop forces in the muscles to move the body; but it is necessary for these forces to be developed at speed so that the body may be moved quickly around the court. A quick player who lacks strength will have only a limited power potential, but equally a strong player who is slow will also lack power.

Agility

This relates to the ability to stop, start, and change direction rapidly and in a controlled manner. Players with good agility will be able to adapt quickly and move into position for shots coming at them from any angle. If you have been wrong-footed by a deceptive opponent, good agility skills will still give you the chance to recover and get back into the correct position for your shot. Players with good agility are generally light on their feet and are often described as having 'quick feet'.

Flexibility

Flexibility is the range of motion about a joint or a series of joints and gives us 'reachability'. If you watch top-level squash you will see numerous examples where a player is required to perform extreme lunging and twisting actions. Without suitable levels of flexibility these actions would not be possible and a player would be more likely to sustain an injury in trying to perform them. For a flexible player even the furthest corners of the court become accessible. For a squash player flexibility around the hips and shoulders is particularly important, along with good rotational ability through the torso.

Body Composition

When talking about body composition we are really interested in the relative proportions of fat and lean tissue which contribute to a player's weight. It is uncommon to see an overweight elite squash player! As we have noted, squash is a weight-bearing sport so that if you have to carry round excess baggage in the form of body fat this will make the game even more demanding than it already is. In the elite game most male players will have body-fat readings of 7 to 12 per cent of body

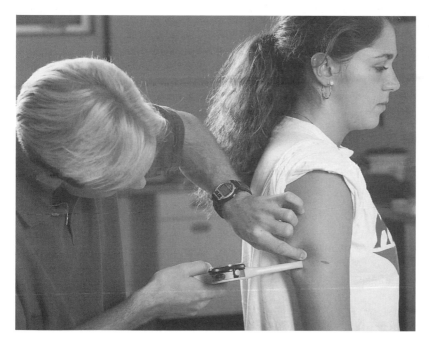

Fig 96 Measuring Campion's body composition.

weight, and the elite women have readings of 18 to 23 per cent. Body-fat levels are influenced by exercise and diet. If you are participating in aerobic exercise on a regular basis and consuming a healthy, balanced diet then your body-fat readings should remain at suitable levels for squash.

Having identified the components of fitness which are needed for success and highlighted the aspects of the game to which they apply, we now need to understand the ways in which we can train to improve these components.

TRAINING TECHNIQUES

Aerobic Fitness

To develop and improve aerobic fitness the two main forms of training which are generally used are:

- steady or continuous intensity training, and
- varied intensity interval training.

To improve aerobic fitness you should first aim to perform at least three sessions a week at an intensity equivalent to 60–90 per cent of your maximum heart rate for at least 20 to 30min duration. Quite simply, this could be performing a 30min run three times a week. It is unlikely you will know your true maximal heart rate unless you have taken part in a performance assessment. As an alternative, you can use as a guide of 220 minus your age to give an age- predicted, maximum heart rate. So if you are a 20-year-old player your age-predicted maximum heart rate would be 200 beats per minute. If you were aiming to work at 75 to 80 per cent of your maximum heart rate during a run then your range would be 150 to 160 beats per minute. Remember that, if you have not

exercised regularly before, then start off at relatively low percentages of your maximum heart rate (60 to 70) and gradually increase the intensity as your fitness progresses.

For continuous intensity training sessions the exercise used is often running since this is a whole-body form of exercise and provides you with the highest heart-rate responses. For variety, you could also use cycling, rowing, swimming or stepping. Most modern gymnasiums have a range of cardiovascular machines that may be used in these training sessions.

Once you have developed a good aerobic base through a consistent period of continuous training, you can then look to include some interval-training sessions in your routine. Interval training involves periods of higher-intensity exercise interspersed with lower-intensity recovery periods. The general premise of interval training is that you should have longer exercise periods than recovery periods, normally a ratio of at least 2:1.

Many of the squash players we have worked with tend to find continuous training mundane and so they will perform long interval sessions for their steady endurance-conditioning work. One advantage of performing this type of session is that it can replicate time periods of exercise similar to those which are required during a game. For example, rather than performing a 30min, steady-paced run a player may choose to perform the session as three 10min runs with a 2min recovery between successive efforts. By performing the session as a series of intervals the player can also work at a slightly higher intensity which is more game-specific. This type of interval session could also be performed using a combination of cardiovascular machines (for instance, 10min cycle ride, 10min run and 10min row).

Higher-intensity interval sessions will involve shorter exercise periods (1 to 5min) and may involve a variety of activities off-court, such as track sessions, hill sprints, cycling or running, in addition to much more specific activities on-court, such as ghosting, sprints and pressure-feeding drills.

A track session could involve sets of 800m sprints completed in less than 3.5min with 2min of jog recovery between efforts, and the completion of five or six sets. The precise distances used, exercise times, recovery times and the number of sets completed will vary according to the capabilities of the individual. Some elite men players will perform sets of 800m in under 2min 45sec, with only 2min of recovery between efforts, and complete from six to eight sets.

Ghosting sessions are an excellent way of improving squash-specific movement endurance capabilities and are widely used by elite players. If aerobic fitness is the primary aim then the movement efforts should be at

least 2min in length. A suitable session could be 2min ghosts with 1min recoveries, performed for between six and ten sets. Ghosting sessions are an excellent way of improving local muscular endurance in addition to general aerobic fitness; however, as we indicated before, if you do not already have a good aerobic base then these sessions will be difficult to complete to any level of quality.

Local Muscular Endurance

Training to improve your muscular endurance will be primarily based around high-intensity interval training and will include a number of the techniques already described for aerobic fitness. The main areas you are trying to target are the muscles in the legs since they have to cope with the repetitive lunging, stopping and starting actions which occur throughout the match. Suitable forms of off-court train-

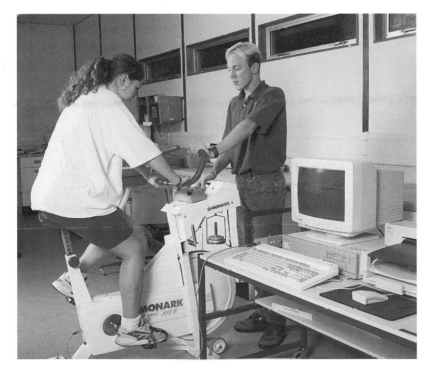

Fig 97
Brown encourages Campion in the body lab.

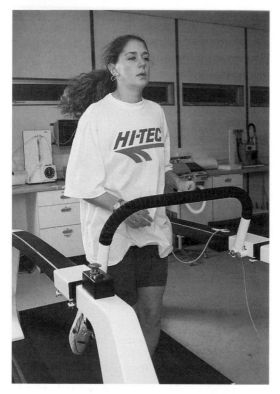

Fig 98 Another 10 miles, please, Cassie!

of 1:1 or 1:2). An elite player with excellent levels of aerobic fitness might use shorter recovery periods as he will have the ability to recover quickly between exercise bouts. An example of a ghosting session to improve muscular endurance would be a 45sec ghost with a 45sec recovery performed for between eight and ten sets. Another useful way of performing muscular endurance sessions would be in the form of a pyramid session with exercise and recovery bouts of varying lengths. The following is an example of a pyramid court sprint session that might be used by an elite player:

Number of sprints	Recovery time (seconds)
10	30
20	45
30	60
40	90
50	90
40	90
30	60
20	45

ing to improve muscular endurance will include track work, hill sprint sessions and interval sessions on the bicycle. Many health clubs also offer classes such as spinning, body pump and circuits, and, depending on the specific content of these classes, they normally provide a good alternative for local muscular endurance conditioning.

On-court training mainly revolves around ghosting or court sprint activities. As discussed previously, ghosting sessions are highly specific and allow a player to focus on movement skills at the same time as improving his muscular endurance. For muscular endurance training, recovery periods are generally of the same length or slightly longer than the exercise periods (that is, a work-to-rest ratio

Speed

Speed in most sports may be broken down into three components:

- starting speed (off the mark)
- acceleration
- absolute speed (maximum).

In squash it is unlikely that a player will ever reach his absolute speed because of the short distances he is moving in. The two most important components of speed for the squash player are start speed, which relates to moving quickly away from the 'T' and in recovery from the shot, and acceleration, the player's ability to pick up speed over a short distance.

Start speed is closely linked in with the ability to develop force at speed. Training to improve start speed will focus on strength work and plyometrics drills, which will be discussed in later sections.

Acceleration can be improved with plyometric and agility drills, but also through speed ghosting and court sprint drills. If you are working on improving speed then any activities should be performed at maximal intensity. This means that the duration of the activity will be relatively short (5 to 10sec), but a long period should be allowed to enable full recovery to occur before subsequent efforts (30 to 60sec). Hill sprint sessions performed over short distances (5 to 20m) may be useful in helping to develop acceleration, as may sprint drills performed on a track.

Skipping may also be a useful activity in helping to develop hand and foot co-ordination while improving speed off the mark.

Strength

The primary aim of strength training is to improve the ability of the muscles to generate force, while also helping to improve the general stability and control of body movements.

The most common forms of training to improve strength involve the use of free weights or the fixed-weights machines that may be found in most well-equipped gymnasiums. The use of your own bodyweight as a resistance can be an effective way of developing strength in the early stages of a programme if you have no former experience in strength training. Remember that it is important that you are able to control your own bodyweight through a range of movements before progressing on to exercises using weights.

Bodyweight exercises can be easily incorporated into a strength-conditioning circuit performed on- or off-court. Suitable bodyweight exercises would be squats, lunges (multidirectional), split squats, walking lunges, press-ups, triceps dips, abdominal and lower-back exercises. Body bars (weighted exercise bars) can be used to increase the intensity of the lower-body drills, and also provide additional upper-body drills, such as shoulder presses and biceps curls.

Once a sufficient strength base has been developed through such exercises, the stimulus for further increases in strength is achieved through the use of free weights and fixed-weight machines to provide additional resistance for the muscles to overcome. Before commencing on any strength training programme you should seek advice from a qualified instructor who will be able to provide guidance on safety and technique and will design a programme to meet your own specific needs.

Fixed-weight machines have the advantage of being generally safer and easier to use than free weights because you are less likely to trip over, be hit by or be trapped under a weight, and they normally require less instruction on technique. In addition, less skill is required to maintain control of a fixed-weight stack than of a free weight. However, this in itself is one of the major disadvantages of fixed machines since they do not place the same demands on the stabilizing muscle groups as free-weights exercises. In squash you are never working muscle groups in isolation but will be performing movements involving the integration and co-ordination of a number of muscle groups to stabilize, support and assist in the movement. Free weights are much more adaptable in their ability to mimic closely sports-specific actions, involving the more natural co-ordination of several muscle groups. Most strength training work performed by elite players will be with free weights, but will be done with supervision and instruction from an experienced instructor.

A range of free-weight exercises that might be included in a squash player's strength programme include back squats, front squats, lunges, step-ups, split squats, bench press, chest flys, reverse flys and shoulder presses. This is not comprehensive and any programme put together should be based around a player's specific needs.

A typical strength session would include from two to four lower body exercises and the same number of upper body exercises. For an inexperienced athlete it is best to start off with high numbers of repetitions of each exercise and low resistances. This pattern provides the player with plenty of opportunities to develop lifting techniques in the early stages. Initially this will help to improve neuromuscular co-ordination and will also lend itself to strength-endurance development. Only when the player is comfortable with the lifting techniques should progress be made on to heavier resistances and fewer repetitions of exercises.

When performing a strength session it is common to alternate between exercises for different body regions (for instance, follow a leg exercise with an upper body exercise), to allow one set of muscle groups to be rested while another is exercised. It is also normal to include the larger muscle-group exercises at the start of a session and finish with smaller muscle-group exercises. For example, squats would come before calf raises, and bench press would come before biceps curls.

It is vital not to forget to train the muscles around the torso as they are extremely important in providing strength and stability during most of the movements you will perform on the squash court. Torso conditioning should involve exercises for the lower back and the abdominals in addition to the stabilizing muscles around the pelvic area. The majority of these exercises are performed using the bodyweight as the resistance, but may be advanced by the use of medicine balls and Swiss balls (inflatable balls used for training core stability). Other forms of training that may be used to help develop strength involve the use of resistance bands or weighted vests.

Power

The main aim of power training is to improve the rate at which force can be deployed in the muscles. Power may be developed through a number of training techniques, including the use of free weights exercises performed at moderate to high speeds, plyometric drills and other resisted exercises incorporating medicine balls, weighted vests and resisted bungees.

The major emphasis of power training with free weights is on speed of movement and the resistances used are typically lower than those used in a traditional strength-training programme. Exercises that could be used for developing power include jump squats with a weighted bar, power step-ups with dumbbells or a bar, bench press exercises with a release performed on a Smith's machine. In addition to the more traditional strength exercises another excellent way of developing power is through the use of explosive Olympic-style lifts with heavy loadings. Olympic lifts include exercises such as power clean, hang clean, clean and jerk and power snatch. Many of these lifts are highly technical in nature and should be performed only by an individual with a solid grounding in strength training and under the supervision of a qualified instructor. When Olympic-style lifts are performed at high speeds with heavy loading the benefits to the player include an increase in maximum strength, an improvement in the rate of force development at moderate to high movement speeds and improved body control.

Plyometric training is another excellent technique for developing explosive power and involves the performing of a series of hopping, bounding or jumping movements. Plyometric training takes advantage of the muscles' natural elastic-recoil properties and is based on the premise that, if the muscle is stretched rapidly before shortening, then the subsequent contraction becomes more forceful and the accompanying movement becomes more dynamic. Plyometrics are performed at high intensity and can be extremely demanding on the muscles and connective tissues around the joints. Before starting any plyometric programme you need a good grounding in strength training since this will help to reduce the risk of injury. Plyometric training should be introduced gradually into your programme as it has the potential to cause high levels of muscle soreness if you overdo it.

The other major form of power training involves performing the movements specific to squash using resistances which are only slightly heavier than those normally used (that is, your own bodyweight). The main focus of this form of training is to improve the speed and acceleration of your movement around court. Elite players perform this form of training wearing weighted vests or resisted bungee cords and work to specific patterns of movement. Exercise periods are normally no more than 15sec in length, with recovery periods of 45sec or more.

Agility

The main aim of agility training is to improve a player's ability to accelerate, decelerate and change direction under control without significant loss in momentum. Agility training also helps a player to develop better control and co-ordination of movement due to an increased kinesthetic awareness of body positioning.

Agility training is based around drills that expose players to rapid changes of direction, movements requiring quick feet and reactive drills which can involve responding to calls made by the coach. The main emphasis should be on good body control during all drills, while performing the movements as fast as possible. A set of floor-marking cones is a good investment since these may be used to mark out drills on court which require movements in all possible directions.

Agility drills are of a short duration (5 to 15sec), with adequate recovery allowed between each drill (30 to 45sec). If a player is working through a session containing many different drills, it may last for up to an hour, but the player should still feel relatively fresh at the end of it.

Flexibility

The main aim of flexibility training is to improve the range of motion about a joint or a series of joints.

Flexibility may take the form of static or dynamic stretches. Static stretching is the most common form performed by squash players, typically in the warm-up to a training session or match and in the warm-down period. Static stretching involves slow movements with the end position being held for a period that may range from 10 to 30sec. Static stretching is typically performed as an active stretch where the player exercising provides the force for the stretch. However, it may also be performed as a passive stretch where a partner provides the force for the stretch. Another form which normally involves a partner is PNF stretching (proprioceptive neuromuscular facilitation). PNF stretching is thought to result in good improvements in the range of motion, but is often impracticable because a certain level of expertise is required as well as a partner.

Stretching following a training session or match may be well timed to facilitate improvements in the range of motion because of the increase in muscle temperature, and thus should normally be performed 5 to 10min after exercise. This increase in temperature leads to increases in the elasticity of the muscles and tendons, therefore allowing for greater increases in stretchability. Stretching after exercise may also help to reduce post-exercise muscle soreness and stiffness. When stretching with the aim of improving the range of motion, stretches should be held for up to 30sec. A stretching programme for a squash player should includes stretches that target the quadriceps, the hamstrings, the hip flexors, the calves, the ankles, the groin, the buttocks, the lower back, the obliques, the shoulders and the upper back. A qualified fitness instructor or sports physiotherapist should be able to put together a comprehensive programme for you.

When stretching is used as part of the warm-up to a training session or match it should include more dynamic stretches in addition to some static stretches. Remember that during static stretching you are stationary and this is not always the best way to prepare your body for the exercise to follow. Dynamic stretching is in essence warming up by using sports-specific movements. The movements performed should help the player to prepare for competition by increasing his sports-specific flexibility. For a squash player this may be as simple as performing some simulated movements (ghosting), starting at a low intensity (walking pace), and then gradually increasing in intensity so that it is close to competition pace. Dynamic stretching could also include some controlled lunging movements and a series of exaggerated swings and twisting movements to increase mobility in the upper body and torso.

CHAPTER 8

The Mind Game

Sport psychology is not just about having a problem, it is about enhancing performance. Sport psychology is taking an ever-increasing role in the squash player's performance. Research has demonstrated that what goes on in the mind can have a significant impact on a player's performance. We have developed beyond identifying the 'problem player' and taken a much broader role in looking at the player as a whole person, accounting for his or her lifestyle and sporting environment. As well, sport psychology focuses on specific mental skills particular to the player; such as motivation in training, anxiety in competition, concentration, emotional control, confidence and self-belief.

Despite the efforts to create an understanding that sport psychology is about enhancing performance, it is still often viewed as crisis-resolving and not crisis-preventing. This chapter is aimed at dispelling this myth, giving the player a better understanding about sport psychology as a tool to train and develop the mind in the same way that he trains and develops the body – it takes time and needs practice. The body and the mind do not exist in isolation. As the body becomes better and better in sport so should the mind. The focus of this chapter will be to highlight the key areas of mental skills specific to squash: motivation and goal setting, concentration and the handling of pressure.

Have you ever woken up on a dark, cold, rainy winter morning and felt like staying in your warm bed rather than going training? Have you ever stood waiting for a serve and thought, 'Why am I here?' or 'Am I really ready for this?' If so you should appreciate the impact that the mind can have during training and before, during and after a match. Sport psychology is about developing the mental skills to turn situations like these, and the potentially negative impact they can have on a performance, into positive experiences where you feel confident, in control and motivated.

As a player, it is important to believe in what you are doing, to understand why you are doing it, to learn from experiences and ultimately to feel that you have done all you can in preparation for a performance. More often than not, players who have succeeded at the highest level refer to a mental edge or toughness that gave them an advantage.

Every committed player will put in the physical miles, but what about the mental miles? Players at all levels dream of winning but there is only ever one winner. The mind has a powerful role in the process of achievement and may ultimately be the major underlying factor in successful performance in the game both during training and in competition. Sport psychology can help all players to get through the daily routines of practising and coping with injury and other setbacks in order ultimately to prepare the player to perform to the best of his ability, and especially on the days that it counts the most.

MOTIVATION

Motivation on and off the court is key to successful training and match play, and the key to motivation is goal achievement. The best way to enhance motivation is to work towards goals that you have set for yourself. Goal setting is about having a vision and supporting that vision with action.

What is your vision? Do you have one? If not, ask yourself where you would like to be one year from now or what you would like to being doing in five years' time. The benefits of goal setting are numerous and everyone in his own way can take advantage of having personal goals. The process of setting goals gives direction and clarity to what you are doing, and, once you know where you are going, there is a tendency to persist in your efforts to get there. Performers with goals succeed because they know where they are going – if you do not know where you are going, how can you get there?

Setting specific goals before training can help to relieve boredom by making the session more challenging, which can improve the quality of your practising. Goal setting can help to ensure regular improvements and ultimately increase the chance of a successful training session and performance. Finally, when you set goals your ultimate aim is to achieve them. Goal achievement instils a tremendous feeling of pride and satisfaction which in turn helps to develop feelings of self-confidence and self-motivation. Goal setting commences a process of being self-reflective and honest with yourself and of identifying areas which need to be developed for you to be a better player.

As the structure of this book indicates, we approach squash coaching in five main areas.

- Technical: refers to the skills involved in squash; for example, the forehand drive.
- Tactical: refers to the strategy associated with executing a task, your game plan.
- Physical: refers to the physiological or fitness aspects of the sport, such as power or speed.
- Mental: refers to the psychological demands of the sport, such as concentration.
- Lifestyle: refers to the way you live your life outside training and competing; for example, the amount of sleep you get every night.

Within each of these five areas there are elements that you can review and from which identify your own strengths and weaknesses; this is both motivating and directing, reflecting on the things you are good at and picking

Your Performance Profile									
Date:_____									
Technical	*Score*	**Tactical**	*Score*	**Physical**	*Score*	**Mental**	*Score*	**Lifestyle**	*Score*
						Concentration			
						Handling pressure			
						Relaxation			
						Using imagery			
						Setting goals			

up on those that need work. It is important here to be honest with yourself to reflect truly where you think you are and where you would like to be. You can analyse your own performance relative to yourself and others with whom you compete. Once you have identified the aspects you need to work on you can begin to set yourself goals and start training specifically towards their improvement. This is your starting point for goal setting.

Use the chart on page 94 to analyse you strengths and weaknesses in each area of training and play. Give yourself a rating – a score out of 10 or 100 – to establish your goals and workloads. If you are honest, it will soon be clear which areas of your game need the greatest attention.

The table overleaf highlights the specific qualities of each type of goal and provides a space to write your own goals.

Don't leave your performance to wishful thinking. Plan to make it happen!

TYPES OF GOAL

There are three main types of goal; these are: outcome, performance and process goals.

Key points:
- Set goals to motivate yourself.
- Set different types of goal: dream, outcome, performance and process.
- Make sure goals are *SMARTER* (specific, measurable, attainable, realistic, time phased, exciting and recorded).

CONCENTRATION

Concentration is the relaxed state of being alert and where your mind is able to focus on the information that is relevant to your playing at that time (for example, being alert

to where your opponent is and not the noise outside the court). When a player is concentrating well he is able to make accurate decisions (shot selection) and effectively execute that shot (with no last-minute changes). Ultimately, total concentration reflects the feeling of being in 'the zone' where you are operating in your ideal performance state: your mind and body are working in harmony, your positive thoughts will produce positive playing and have positive results.

Key points:
- Know what the important cues are and be able to selectively focus on these.
- Keep thoughts positive and technically correct.

Distractions are a prime cause of poor concentration. We are often easily distracted when we are nervous and fatigued. There are two types of distraction: *external*, such as noise from the crowd, verbal comments from the crowd, movement behind the court, the temperature of the court and poor lighting; and *internal*, such as remembering a previous error, worrying about the next rally, or an injury reoccurring, over analysis or anger with a refereeing decision. Identify what distracts you:

Distractions	
Internal	External

Develop your Concentration

Try to identify with key elements and use them to refocus your thoughts when you feel your concentration slipping; these may be words or phrases, an image or a physical

Types of Goal			
Type of Goal	Definition	Examples	Your Goals
Dream	Where you would ultimately aim to achieve in the future, where you would love to be ...	Winning the national championship ... in three years' time.	
Outcome	● These goals reflect the outcome or end result of a competitive situation; that is, you win or lose a match. ● Outcome goals can often have a long-term aspect to them; that is, a tournament result or season result. ● These goals are not always in your control since on the day your opponent may be better than you. ● Outcome should not be the only focus of your attention while playing. ● Outcome goals are exciting and are often what you are constantly striving for when you are training and competing.	Winning a club closed tournament.	
Performance (what do I want to achieve?)	● Performance goals focus on the 'what': what do I need to do to improve my squash? ● Performance goals often reflect the medium- to short-term period and feed into outcome goals. ● Performance goals are the goals that are in your control; achieving a performance goal is down to you and your personal improvement regardless of others. These goals might reflect a timed run or accuracy of shot placement on court during a match. ● The performance goal should be measurable in order to see improvements.	Improve my club ranking by reaching top five next year and club number one in two years.	

continued on page 97

Type of Goal	Definition	Examples	Your Goals
Process (how am I going to achieve it?)	• Process goals focus on the 'how': how am I going to do this? • Process goals underpin performance goals and are key to success: without process goals the achieving of performance and outcome goals is limited. • They are what you do on a day-to-day basis to get the most out of your squash, such as quality training sessions, rest and attention to nutrition. • The key here is to keep asking yourself: How am I going to do this?	Start taking coaching from a qualified coach; increase training from 2 to 3 evenings per week and record all training activities	

behaviour that you can relate to. The most obvious example is your game plan. Assuming you have one, you can then instantly refer to the things you planned to do and use those thoughts to regain concentration. Other examples may be single words such as 'ready' and 'relax' or technical words such as 'length'. You might also choose to focus intently on something you can see in or around the court, such as the tin, the door or your racket. Finally, you may prefer to do something physical to refocus yourself, such as wipe your hand on the wall, walk up to the front of the court and back, take a deep breath or jump lightly up and down on your toes.

Similarly key points of focus are useful for *error parking*; that is, effectively getting rid of the mistake after it has been made. If you find it difficult to get errors out of your mind and you find yourself dwelling on the mistake you can attempt to use your focus cues to put it behind you. Give your mind something else to focus on, not the mistake. A further way of developing your concentration is to simulate the competitive match environment. When possible, and to the best of your ability, create a situation that replicates the sorts

of distraction you might find yourself in during a match, such as noise, verbal insults, conditioned games or unfavourable conditions to challenge your concentration. By exposing yourself to these situations you hope to become more tolerant of the distractions and to stay focused. It is difficult to reproduce and to do justice to the 'real thing', but attempting to simulate the match or tournament environment can definitely help to train the mind to maintain concentration effectively.

In using your key points of focus you are preventing a blank mind from embracing any negativity or worry. You may choose to use only one type of focus or a combination of all of them. A key component to all of this is *belief*. You must believe in the words, phrases or images that you choose in order to allow them to be effective in focusing your attention on what is relevant to your game at that moment. This also means that the player is in control of identifying what works best for him. It is a very individual process.

Key points:
• Identify key words, phrases, imagery or actions that work for you.

97

- Use these key elements to refocus if your concentration is slipping.
- Use these key elements to recover from a mistake.
- Create an environment, when possible, to replicate the competitive match situation.

HANDLING PRESSURE

At all levels of squash, when you are faced with an opponent of similar ability, one of the key factors separating the winner from the loser is likely to be the player's ability to cope with pressure. Some players naturally thrive under the pressure of competition more than others. For many the ability to use the pressure positively to enhance their squash is a difficult and challenging prospect. Handling pressure before, during and often after a match, and even during a training session, may be an overwhelming obstacle. The challenge for any player is being able to interpret a potentially negative or threatening situation in a positive and challenging way. Many players never achieve their potential because they frequently allow the occasion to get the better of them. Pressure situations, where expectations are high and where the fear of failure can suddenly take over, can negatively affect any player and prevent him from playing to the best of his ability.

There is nothing unusual about feeling nervous. It exists and all players, as well as coaches, will experience it in varying degrees. Stress occurs when there is an imbalance between what is being asked of you and your belief that you have the ability to do it. If we feel that we have not got the ability to deal with a situation then we feel stress. If we feel that we can achieve the task then we may still feel stress, but a stress of a more positive and excited nature than worry.

An important factor in how we deal with stress is how it is interpreted. That is, some players will perceive a potentially stressful situation as a challenge; for example, 'Great that I get to play the county No.1 in the first round', while others are more prone to experience the same situation as a threat; for instance, 'Oh no, I have to play the county No.1 in the first round.' If a potentially stressful situation is viewed as a challenge then the player or coach is more inclined to feel excited by it. Whereas if the situation is seen as a threat the individual will doubt his ability and feel worried. Stress affects players differently and different situations may have differing effects on the same player.

Some players find that they get very nervous before a match and this helps them to play well. For others the stress of the situation prevents them from playing in the way that they would like to. Some players may find that they do not become nervous at all and this helps them to achieve, while others may get into the first game, not feel up to it and thus underperform.

What happens when we experience stress? It can affect us mentally, which is usually identified as worry, self-doubt, team doubt, lack of concentration or changes in perception. For example, pre-match, wondering whether your family or friends have arrived, worrying about whether you are going to have a good game; doubting during play whether you can play a certain shot, or remembering a mistake from a previous game or your last match. A player can also experience stress physically, such as excessive muscle tension, butterflies or a retching sensation in the stomach, sweaty palms, jelly legs or feeling tired. Finally, stress can have an effect on our behaviour. Pre-match, not sleeping the night before, not eating, becoming more talkative or going totally quiet. Post-match, forget to have your usual debrief and just walk away from the match.

The different ways in which stressful situations have an impact on the player and coach are too many to count. However, the key is being able to identify with yourself, as the player or the coach, the way you want to feel and behave before, during and after the match or practice; and then attempting to interpret stressful situations as challenges and using the new skills or tools to control your levels of stress to enhance your performance.

To assist a player to develop optimal effective coping strategies it helps first to identify what causes the stress and then develop mental, physical and behavioural ways to deal with it. Many factors may have an effect on a player. These may be experienced during training, in the lead up to a match, during the knock-up and during the match. It may help to list the possible problem areas as in the table below.

COPING STRATEGIES

There are just as many ways of dealing with stress. Here are a few.

Going Straight to the Source

If you can identify what is actually causing the stress you can temporarily relieve it by putting some perspective on it and even

possibly prevent it from reappearing in the future. We have discussed likely sources of stress above; very often reducing stress at its source is about controlling the controllables – reducing uncertainty, and planning. For example, being able to put the referee's decision behind you because you cannot control his decision, knowing about the opposition, or leaving yourself enough time to get to the match.

Interpret the Situation as a Challenge Rather than a Threat

All players will interpret stressful situations differently. Some will see a particular situation as challenging while others may feel threatened by it. No matter how hard you try to prepare for a match or tournament your ability as a player or coach to address or deal with all the eventualities which may occur on the day is limited. There will always be those circumstances that create stress simply because they are not expected or are out of your control. The challenge is being able to view the situation positively rather than negatively when under pressure – viewing it as a challenge rather than a threat is critical.

Our reasons for appraising information differently may be a consequence of past experiences (did one of the players hear some

Factors Impacting on Performance		
Internal Factors	**External Factors**	**Your Own**
Importance of the match	Court conditions	
Perceived ability of opposition	Distractions: family, friends, crowd (for instance, during the match)	
Previous match performance (lack of self-belief)	Travel and disruption to your routine	
Carrying an old injury or first time back after injury	Referee decisions	
Staying motivated during training and playing season	Others' expectations (for instance, pre-match)	

distressing news moments before arriving at the club?), general mood (didn't sleep well the night before), did not play well against this person last time, or noticed for the first time a large crowd as he stepped on court. Furthermore, if you feel that the demand you face is beyond your capability and that perhaps the result will have serious consequences, you will feel more open to a threatening appraisal.

Can you convert negative thoughts and feelings into a more positive mindset? Can you use the stressful situation to create an exciting and motivating performance because of the way you think about it? The catchphrase 'When the going gets tough, the tough get going' demonstrates this. In order to make the most of every competitive situation it is vital that the player's appraisal or reappraisal of the situation is seen as a positive step and that he uses stress to his advantage. The essence of positive perspective is being able to challenge your irrational thinking. In the table below are some examples of players' being able to reconstruct irrational thoughts to make them rational, positive and challenging.

In an attempt to view a difficult situation, positive thinking can have a powerful impact. This can be done through positive affirmations and self-talk for general and specific squash situations.

Positive self-talk refers to the player's ability to identify and concentrate on words, phrases and sometimes images which bring feelings of confidence and control. This is not always an easy process as we tend to pick on our faults more often than our strengths and sometimes contribute to our own downfall. However, when you have identified your own words, phrases or images these can act as a buffer to negative thoughts. This helps to keep you focused and positive about yourself, your ability and your performance. Stay focused on how you are going to succeed rather than the success itself. Positive thinking on the task at hand helps to keep the mind focused on the present, the here and now. If you have a positive mental self-image and perception of your ability these traits lead to confidence and a good performance rather than negativity, doubt and worry, leading to a decline in performance.

Give Yourself Performance Routines

Pre-match and pre-performance routines give a sense of familiarity and calmness when under pressure. Pre-match routine refers to a flexible but planned step-by-step process the player can go through in preparation for a match and even a training session. Most players have an idea of the sorts of routine they like to do before playing. This is commendable, but can you remember the important detail from match to match, month after month? When you have had a successful performance, would you not wish to remember what you did to prepare for it and recall some of the detail that may have made the difference?

Changing Negative to Positive	
Irrational Thought	Rational Thinking
I'll never beat him.	I am on a roll, I am coming off the back of two great performances, I am going to take the ball early.
I never play well against him; he winds me up.	I am going to concentrate on my own game plan and I am ready for it.
My backhand volley is appalling.	Stay relaxed and take my time – no rushing.

Try to avoid leaving preparation to chance. Take time to reflect on your match when it is over, perhaps write a few points down so that you do not have to rely on memory. By considering a pre-match routine you can be in control of putting yourself in the right frame of mind before you play. Pre-performance routines focus on the steps you take before carrying out an action such as serving. Routines are effective when you have time on your side to prepare for what you are about to do rather than rushing and leaving the outcome to chance.

A player might perform the routines set out in the table below.

Familiarization is another way to prepare and take comfort in the surrounding area and the court on which you are playing. When it is possible, arrive early to check the facilities and become familiar with the court. Finding out some specific information about the venue can become part of your pre-match routine preparation.

Key points:
● Routines help to block out irrelevant distractions by providing a focus for your attention.
● Routines provide a sense of familiarity and calm.
● Routines provide a solid framework in which to use your skills; they lead to consistency and enhance confidence.

Learning to Use Relaxation

Our bodies react differently to attacks of 'nerves', such as by butterflies in the stomach, jelly-like legs, sweaty palms, shaking hands, an increase in the heart rate and faster breathing – these are all physical responses to stress. Different forms of physical and mental relaxation can help with nerves the night before a match, pre-match, and during the match.

The techniques you use will depend on personal preference and the timing of the exercise in relation to the start of the match. In general, breathing and relaxation techniques help to control nervous energy. Greater controls may help a player to sleep better, especially in the lead-up to a big match, prepare the mind and body for imagery training, improve concentration and can help to improve overall bodily awareness. There are different techniques for controlling your breathing and for physical relaxation. Two common breathing techniques are focused breathing and centring, and a physical technique known as progressive muscle relaxation (PMR). These help to reduce nervous tension by lowering the heart rate and reducing muscle tension, allowing the player to feel in control of his body.

Preparation Routines		
Pre-Match Routine	Pre-Performance (Serve)	Post-Match Routine
Arrival time at the club, getting changed, warm-up (knowing what you like to do in the warm-up and for how long).	Foot placement, deep breath, bouncing the ball three times, pausing and knowing what type of serve you want to play. better?	Approximately 2hr after the match take time to make a few comments to yourself about your match: What went well? What could have been

Fig 99 Kirsten Barnes (centre) leads the team's analysis of the success of Jenny Duncalf (second right) in the European Junior Final in Amsterdam.

CONTROLLED BREATHING

Focused Breathing

Find a comfortable place in which to sit or lie down, with feet uncrossed and hands on your stomach. Make sure you are comfortable and generally feeling fully relaxed. Begin breathing in through your nose and out through your mouth. Each breath should be deep, using your diaphragm. With your hands resting on your stomach, you should be able to feel your stomach rising and falling with each breath. Try to focus all your attention on the centre of your body and feel your stomach muscles expand and relax. Now you can introduce counting to your breathing to slow it down even more. As you take deep breaths count to yourself as you inhale (in, 2, 3, 4) and exhale (out, 2, 3, 4); repeat this counting pattern to help to slow your heart rate. You may also find that you have a particular word that helps you relax, such as 'relax' or 'calm', which you can introduce to your thoughts once you have established a steady, slow, rhythmical, deep-breathing pattern. Now you should be feeling an all-over sense of relaxation. This technique is particularly useful to help you fall asleep at night, especially if you are feeling anxious about a match.

Centring

This is a shortened version of focused breathing which you might use before going on court and then while playing. Again, it operates on the principle that, by taking a moment to take in more oxygen and slow your breathing down and lower your heart rate, you start to release muscle tension, and you are putting yourself in a better playing state. Centring involves the process of taking a few deep breaths while sitting or standing, which allows your body to feel in control and relaxed but not in a deep form of focused breathing relaxation. Concentrate your attention on your stomach and feel slow, deep breaths coming from your diaphragm, feel your abdomen moving out as you breathe in through your nose. As you breathe, feel relaxation in your muscles, and as you exhale feel the tension leave your muscles. When you are ready, stand up and shake yourself out, feeling relaxed and energized. This is also a good time to use a cue word, phrase or image to refocus your thoughts direct on the task at hand, such as concentrating on the serve.

The PMR Technique

Progressive muscle relaxation is a technique which distinguishes the tense muscle from the relaxed muscle. The exercise follows on well from the focused breathing when the body is feeling relaxed and you want to feel even more so. This is a good exercise to do before

Fig 100 Kirsten Barnes, an Olympic Gold Medalist for Canada in Rowing, who is sports psychologist for England's successful World Class Performance.

going to sleep, especially if you have trouble sleeping on the night before a game.

How to do it: while sitting or lying comfortably, take some deep breaths and feel an overall relaxation. Focusing your attention on your feet, tighten up all the muscles in your feet and hold (count 1, 2) and then relax the muscles. Repeat this twice more. Then move to your calf muscles and hold as before, relax and repeat. Then move up to your quads, gluts, the stomach and then out to the hands, forearms, upper arms, shoulders, neck and face; again hold, relax and repeat as before. Try to isolate the particular muscle groups, although this is not easy, but it helps to increase your awareness of the major muscles in your body and the tension that may exist from pressure. You can modify the exercise as you become familiar with it; for example, you can tense and relax all the muscles in your legs at once then progress through the middle part of your body, the upper body and then the face.

MOVEMENT

Another way to allow tension to leave your muscles is by actually moving them around. Your physical warm-up off and on court should be seen as a good opportunity to relieve nervous tension. If you have been driving to the venue, waiting around before the match or rushed on to court, you will want to activate yourself physically and mentally. A light jog or short running bursts or stretching simply to elevate the heart and the breathing rate can create an energized feeling to switch your mind and body into playing mode and help to dispel an excess of nervous energy. While activating yourself you may find that listening to music also helps you either to get switched on or to take your mind off the match.

IMAGERY

Using imagery is also a good way to cope with nerves and prepare yourself for a match or training session. Imagery is the act of seeing yourself clearly in your mind's eye playing any aspect of the game, feeling yourself playing, feeling the racket in your hand and your movement on the court. In preparation for playing, imagery is useful to (1) familiarize yourself with the venue (especially if it is your first time there) and (2) to calm yourself by imagining a place that you find quite comforting or (3) where you rehearse your warm-up or other aspects of the game to get yourself focussed.

TIME ON YOUR OWN

When you are playing in a team it is easy to find yourself constantly surrounded by team members and never feeling like you have time for yourself. If being alone is important to you it is crucial that you create time to be on your own during an event, and especially when you are preparing to play. You might want to think about the things you like to do on your own before you leave home or work, and remember to take with you the necessary items that you need. For example, it may mean a book, magazines, music or games, or talking to friends outside squash that really helps you – anything that allows you to create time for yourself, especially if you are feeling particularly nervous. Use your pre-competition routines to help to map out the time you will spend preparing on your own and when you want to be with others such as team members.

BODY LANGUAGE

When you are nervous you often look it. Negative body language is informaiton for

104

your opponent. Think about your body language. If you see someone walking around with his head down, shoulders drooping and pacing up and down, your first thoughts may be 'He looks nervous.' This is not a confident message to be sending out to your opponent. Think about your own self-presentation; you too might be feeling nervous inside but that does not mean that you have to show it. Walk with conviction, head up, shoulders back, be quick to refocus after a mistake, get into position and be ready for the next rally.

SUMMARIZED KEY POINTS

- Go to the source of stress, if possible, to relieve it.

- Interpret pressure situations as challenges not threats.
- Use pre-match and pre-performance routines to prepare and stay calm under pressure.
- Use relaxation and imagery techniques to stay in control, switch off and mentally prepare.
- Find time for yourself, if necessary, when preparing to play.
- Adopt positive body language – attitude not arrogance.

There is nothing magical or mysterious about sport psychology and mental skills. However, they may make the difference to your performance some day. A critical underlying factor to any successful sporting experience is having confidence in your own ability and

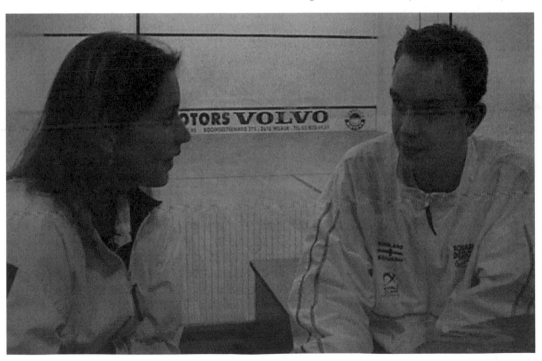

Fig 101 Kirsten Barnes with British Junior Champion James Willstrop before his European Junior Final in Amsterdam.

believing that you can achieve what you set out to do. Developing your mental skills, such as the ones described in this chapter, will help to give you more confidence and belief in your ability as a player. It is worth giving your mental performance some consideration as you develop and integrate the training of your mind, as you do of your body, into your daily experiences in playing squash.

Useful Addresses

World Squash Federation (WSF)
6 Havelock Road
Hastings
East Sussex
TN34 1BP
England
Tel: (44) 1424 429245
Fax: (44) 1424 429250
E-mail: www.worldsquash.org

Squash Federation of Africa
PO Box 613
Northlands
2116 Transvaal
South Africa
Tel: (27) 11 442 8056
Fax: (27) 11 442 8036
E-mail: jan@squashsa.co.za

Asian Squash Federation
Dhun Building
3rd Floor
North Wing
827 Anna Selai
Chennai 600 002
India
Tel: (91) 44855 0254
Fax: (91) 44 852 0717
E-Mail: finance@md2.vsnl.net.in

European Squash Federation
6 Havelock Road
Hastings

East Sussex
TN34 1BP
England
Tel: (44) 1424 428299
Fax: (44) 1424 429 250
E-mail: sue@european-squash.org.uk

Federation PanAmerican De Squash
Calle 9 42–55 Of.201, A>A> 10045
Medellin
Columbia
Tel: (57) 4 268 0911/268 9999
Fax: (57) 4 268 8001
E-mail: sergio@epm.net.co

Oceania Squash Federation
23 Kinsella Street
Belmont Heights
Queensland 4153
Australia
Tel: (61) 7 32245903
Fax: (61) 7 33906694
E-mail: clapper@powerup.com.au

Squash England
Belle Vue Athletics Centre
Pink Bank Lane
Manchester
M12 5GL
England
Tel: (44) 161 231 4499
Fax: (44) 161 231 4231
E-mail: sra@squash.co.uk

USEFUL ADDRESSES

Scottish Squash
Caledonian House
South Gyle
Edinburgh
EH12 9DQ
Tel: (44) 131 317 7343
Fax: (44) 131 317 7734
E-mail: scottishsquash@aol.com

Irish Squash
House of Sport
Long Mile Road
Dublin 12
Ireland
Tel: (353) 1 450 1564
Fax: (353) 1 450 2805
E-mail: irishsquash@eircom.net

Squash Wales
St Mellons Country Club
Cardiff
CF2 8XR
Wales
Tel: (44) 1633 682108
Fax: (44) 1633 608998
E-mail: squash.wales@tesco.net

Hong Kong Squash
23 Cotton Tree Drive
Hong Kong
Tel: (852) 2869 0611
Fax: (852) 2869 0118
E-mail: hksquash@hkstar.com

Squash Australia
Sports House
Office 9
Cnr Castlemaine & Caxton Streets
Milton
Queensland
QLD 4064
Australia

Tel: (61) 7 3367 3200
Fax: (61) 7 3367 3320
E-mail: squashoz@squash.org.au

Squash New Zealand
PO Box 21–781
Henderson
Auckland
New Zealand
Tel: (64) 9 836 2217
Fax: (64) 9 836 0309
E-mail: squashnz@squashnz.co.nz

Squash Canada
1600 James Naismith Drive
Gloucester
Ontario
K1B 5N4
Canada
Tel: (1) 613–748 5672
Fax: (1) 613–748 5861
E-mail: squashca@home.com

United States Squash Racquets
Association
23 Cynwyd Road
PO Box 1216
Bala Cynwyd
PA 19004
USA
Tel: (1) 610 667 4006
Fax: (1) 610 667 6539
E-mail: ussraexdir@earthlink.net

Squash South Africa
PO Box 613
Northlands
2116
South Africa
Tel: (27) 11 442 8056
Fax: (27) 11 442 8036
E-mail: jan@squashsa.co.za

Professional Squash Association (PSA)
82 Cathedral Road
Cardiff
CF1 9LN
Wales
Tel; (44) 2920 388446
Fax: (44) 2920 228185
E-mail: psa@psacdf.demon.co.uk

Women's International Squash Players
Association (WISPA)
27 Westminster Palace Gardens
Artillery Row
London
SW1 1RR
England
Tel: (44) 207 222 1667
Fax: (44) 207 976 8778
E-mail: wispahq@aol.com

THE BEST OF THE WEBSITES:

www.squashnow.com

www.worldsquash.org

www.squashtalk.com

www.squashpics.com

www.squashplayer.com

Index